TIME

Nature's Wonders

The science and splendor of Earth's most fascinating places

Saline scene *Tufa formations—solidified calcium carbonate deposits—tower over California's Mono Lake*

Rising above it *Shiprock in Mexico, a sacred site to the Navajo, towers 1,583 ft. (482 m) over the surface of the high desert plain. Composed of igneous rock, the kind produced by volcanic eruptions, it is believed to have formed in the throat of a volcano but was never expelled by an eruption. It was exposed by erosion over thousands of years*

TIME

MANAGING EDITOR Richard Stengel
DEPUTY MANAGING EDITORS Michael Elliott, Adi Ignatius, Romesh Ratnesar

Nature's Wonders

EDITOR Kelly Knauer
DESIGNER Ellen Fanning
PICTURE EDITOR Patricia Cadley
WRITER/RESEARCH DIRECTOR Matthew McCann Fenton
COPY EDITOR Bruce Christopher Carr

TIME INC. HOME ENTERTAINMENT
PUBLISHER Richard Fraiman
GENERAL MANAGER Steven Sandonato
EXECUTIVE DIRECTOR, MARKETING SERVICES Carol Pittard
DIRECTOR, RETAIL & SPECIAL SALES Tom Mifsud
DIRECTOR, NEW PRODUCT DEVELOPMENT Peter Harper
ASSISTANT DIRECTOR, BRAND MARKETING Laura Adam
ASSOCIATE COUNSEL Helen Wan
SENIOR BRAND MANAGER, TWRS/M Holly Oakes
BOOK PRODUCTION MANAGER Suzanne Janso
DESIGN AND PREPRESS MANAGER Anne-Michelle Gallero
SENIOR BRAND MANAGER Joy Butts
BRAND MANAGER Shelley Rescober

SPECIAL THANKS
Alexandra Bliss, Glenn Buonocore, Susan Chodakiewicz, Margaret Hess,
Robert Marasco, Dennis Marcel, Brooke Reger, Mary Sarro-Waite, Ilene
Schreider, Adriana Tierno, Alex Voznesenskiy

We welcome your comments and suggestions about TIME Books. Please write
to us at: TIME Books • Attention: Book Editors • PO Box 11016 • Des Moines, IA
50336-1016

If you would like to order any of our hardcover Collector's Edition books,
please call us at 1-800-327-6388 (Monday through Friday, 7 a.m.–8 p.m.,
or Saturday, 7 a.m.–6 p.m., Central time).

PRINTED IN THE UNITED STATES OF AMERICA

Photography credits

Front-cover: Tim Fitzharris—Minden Pictures

Back-cover, top to bottom: Per-Andre Hoffmann—Aurora Photos;
Craig Tuttle—Corbis; Travelpix Ltd.—Getty Images; Norbert Wu—
Getty Images; Jim Brandenburg—Minden Pictures

DANNY LEHMAN—CORBIS

Contents

Crop circles *Cultivated fields of canola surround cone-shaped outcroppings of hard rock around Guizhou, China. In karst topographies like this one, softer rocks have been eroded by weather, but harder ones are still undergoing erosion*

One more layer *A fresh dusting of snow covers Arizona's Grand Canyon*

Introduction

Steep Learning Curve

ASNOWY DAY AT THE GRAND CANYON COMBINES one of Planet Earth's most breathtaking sights with one of its more routine meteorological events—routine, that is, for those who live in wintry climes. It all makes for a scene worthy of a postcard, but that's not why we chose this photograph to introduce a book titled *Nature's Wonders.* The reason is something you won't see in the picture but will read about in these pages: since our editorial team began working on this book, the Grand Canyon got a lot older, and an average snowfall got a lot livelier.

Well, something like that, anyway. Here's what really happened: as this book was in progress, two teams of scientists, a group that had been researching the age of the Grand Canyon and another that had been studying the composition of snow, released their latest findings in respected scientific journals. Their reports made news, and soon scholars, textbook writers, Wikipedia contributors and our editorial group got busy, revising their entries on two of nature's fascinating phenomena.

The Grand Canyon didn't get older, of course, nor did snow change its, uh, spots. It was our understanding of them that changed. The scientists working on the age of the canyon, using advanced radiometric dating techniques, discovered that the great gash carved in the desert plain by the Colorado River is actually 11 million years older than we had previously thought.

The team working on the nature of snow supported a significantly new view of the planet's precipitation cycle that had previously been advanced in theory but never fully established by research. Studying flakes of snow in locations around the globe, the scientists discovered that airborne bacteria are a key coalescing agent that helps water vapor suspended in clouds condense into snowflakes or raindrops. In other words, snow—a part of nature's precipitation cycle, which irrigates the globe—is also linked to the biological cycle in the form of bacteria. This discovery was a fresh reminder of the grand, interwoven complexity of the systems that support life on the planet.

Those systems are the subject of this book. We have classified them according to an ancient way of viewing our world first proposed by the Greeks, who divided the planet's functions into a series of spheres. The outer sphere is the atmosphere that envelops Earth. The hydrosphere, or water system, irrigates the planet, while the pedosphere is the land we walk upon. The geosphere is the subterranean world beneath our feet, an unseen realm whose power we glimpse in earthquakes, volcanoes and tsunamis. Modern scientists have added another world to this group: the cryosphere, or frozen world. Another sphere, the biosphere, composes the world of living things: it will be the subject of a companion book to this volume.

Nature's Wonders explores these spheres, focusing on both the more representative and more extreme of the sights to be seen on nature's various stages. It also explores Earth's natural processes: rain and snow, erosion and tectonic drift, solar winds and spring tides. Not all our explanations are complete, for it is surprising how much we have yet to discover about even the most basic aspects of our planet and its workings, from the age of a canyon to the nature of snow. Our knowledge of the planet we call home is still under construction, but then again, as the stories in this book make clear, so is our wonder-filled planet.

—*Kelly Knauer*

atmosphere

at·mos·phere *(n.)*
[Gk *atmos* vapor + Gk *sphaira* ball]
a gaseous mass enveloping a heavenly body (as a planet
or satellite); the world of the air

Smudges *Morning fog made up of condensing water vapor cloaks a rain forest in Borneo*

The Blue Cocoon

OF ALL NATURE'S WONDERS, PERHAPS THE MOST wonderful is something that often is invisible and is almost always taken for granted: the atmosphere, the cocoon of gases that envelops the planet and makes life possible. All of human history (until very recently, with the advent of space travel) and all phenomena associated with the globe's climate and weather have taken place in this relatively thin layer of gases, which can be seen as a ribbon of blue swaddling the planet in this NASA photograph. The atmosphere serves our world as a kind of celestial moat, a protective barrier that shields Earth from the damaging ultraviolet rays of the sun and also from the potentially harmful impact of the some 1.4 million small meteoroids that burn up and vaporize as they come in contact with it each day.

The crater-scarred surface of the moon, whose atmosphere is very thin, is a chilling reminder of what our planet might look like were it not for the atmosphere. And the extinction of the dinosaurs, now believed to have been caused by the impact of an enormous object that barreled into the planet some 65 million years ago, is a reminder that some asteroids are too large to be consumed by the planet's airy buffer zone.

Earth's vast ocean of air extends, if thinly, to some 430 miles above the planet's surface, where it merges with outer space. It is composed of gases such as nitrogen, oxygen, argon, carbon dioxide and water vapor, as well as the host of small, wind-borne liquid and solid particles that scientists call aerosols: dust and soil, pollen, ash from volcanoes, sea salts made airborne by breaking waves. It is these particulates that turn the sunset red and orange, when the rays of the sun strike Earth through a thick swath of the atmosphere as the star declines to the horizon.

Nitrogen and oxygen make up 99% of the atmosphere; yet the carbon dioxide that composes only some 0.03% of air is the focus of grave scientific concern. Carbon dioxide (CO_2) and water vapor are greenhouse gases; like the panes of glass on a greenhouse, these gases allow solar heat to pass through the atmosphere but trap it inside. As the amount of CO_2 in the air grows, largely owing to the burning of fossil fuels, the resulting gradual heating of the planet is driving unpredictable climate change. ∎

Orb of air *The atmosphere, which is most often seen by humans in the form of a red sunset or smog, is clearly seen as a ribbon of blue surrounding the planet in this 1999 photo*

Air's Layers

Scientists divide the planet's atmosphere into four distinct strata:

Troposphere: The lowest layer of the planet's blue cocoon is *our* layer: the ocean of air in which humans and animals live and weather events occur. It extends upward from the surface of the planet for 12 miles; temperatures drop as the distance from Earth increases and the air thins. The troposphere's thickness changes with the seasonal position of the planet relative to the sun.

Stratosphere: The next layer of the atmosphere extends to 31 miles above the planet. Oxygen here is far too scarce to support life—but temperatures actually increase in the higher regions of the troposphere, for this is where the ozone layer lies, and ozone heats up as it absorbs the sun's harmful ultraviolet rays.

Mesosphere: The third layer of the atmospheric onion extends 53 miles above the planet. Beyond the reach of research balloons, it is a relatively unexplored region of the atmosphere.

Thermosphere: The atmosphere's highest layer—made visible by auroras—extends to the verge of outer space, some 430 miles above Earth. Its thin air composes a tiny fraction of the atmosphere's total mass.

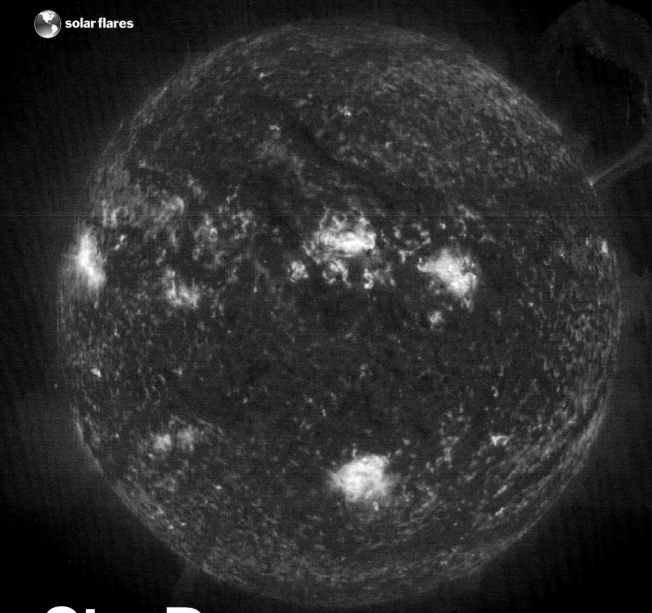

Star Power

THE SUN MAKES LIFE ON EARTH POSSIBLE, YET THE relationship between our planet and the star we revolve around is both so intricate and so all-pervasive that some of its aspects can easily be overlooked. Night and day, the seasons, the climate, the atmosphere, the tides: all these elemental facets of life on Earth reflect our dependence on the sun. Consider solar flares, or prominences, the phenomena captured memorably in the picture above.

A solar flare amounts to a gigantic eruption of the ionized gases, or plasma, that make up the surface of the sun, where the daily forecast typically calls for temperatures of 9-10,000°F. Some solar flares are hundreds of thousands of miles long, so vast as to straddle the distance between the Earth and the moon. Flares are only the most spectacular display of a process that is constantly taking place within the sun: the emission

of charged, or ionized, particles from the star in the form of solar wind. When these particles reach Earth, they can light up polar skies in the form of auroras.

Solar flares, like the magnetic storms we call sunspots and all the other activity on the sun, peak in an 11-year cycle, for reasons we do not yet fully understand. At such times, the sun's charged particles can play havoc with mankind's more advanced systems. In 1989 a massive solar flare disrupted Canada's power grid, shutting it down in some areas and putting all sorts of radio-activated devices on the fritz. Homeowners in Toronto who watched their garage doors opening and closing over and over again for no visible reason may have directed their ire at their local utility provider but should instead have blamed old Sol. The nearest star may make life on Earth possible, but as the Bible reminds us, the sun also fries us. ■

A Starry Crown

At left, a giant solar prominence erupts on Sept. 14, 1999, in an ultraviolet image recorded by the SOHO *spacecraft (Solar and Heliospheric Observatory). The white areas in the image are the hottest. Below, the sun's corona is seen during the last stages of a total solar eclipse on June 21, 2001. The corona, always present but only visible from Earth during eclipses, is made up of plasma, charged particles, and is 200 times hotter than the surface of the sun, for reasons not yet fully explained. Solar flares and coronal activity peak on an 11-year cycle; 2001 was the last peak. The image has been slightly enhanced to make the corona more visible and to simulate its appearance to the naked eye.*

becomes increasingly powerful across the star's entire surface during "solar max" periods

Visions in the Sky

A NYONE FORTUNATE ENOUGH TO HAVE WITNESSED A FULL-ON DISPLAY OF THE AURORA BOREALIS is likely to tell you that the northern lights are among nature's most breathtaking wonders, as are their southern counterparts, the aurora australis. Generally only visible in regions closest to the North and South poles—for reasons detailed in the sidebar at right—the two polar auroras at their best are staggeringly beautiful, rainbows on steroids. Yet in addition to their eerie, iridescent splendor, the auroras are also among the largest and grandest of Earth's wonders visible to the naked eye. These natural light shows illuminate the sheer scale of the planet, beaming across hundreds of thousands of miles of the thermosphere to bring this vast, normally invisible highest region of the atmosphere into sudden, bewitching focus.

Most often shimmering like curtains but at other times beaming like the rays from a giant flashlight, the auroras have transfixed viewers since the dawn of history. The folktales of many northern-dwelling peoples associate the auroras with various mythological entities. Finns believed their light was generated by fiery foxes; other hungry Scandinavians thought they were the reflections of vast schools of herring; Algonquin Indians saw them as departed ancestors dancing around a fire; ancient Scots called the lights *na fir-chlis*, "merry dancers."

Only since the first years of the 20th century have scientists, led by Norwegian physicist Kristian Birkeland, begun to explain the complex celestial mechanisms that create auroras. The process begins with the solar wind, the constant flow of ionized gases, or plasma, that is emitted in all directions by the sun. When these electrically charged particles flow into Earth's magnetic field, or magnetosphere, they are excited and emit energy in the form of colored light. The auroras peak in unison with the sun's 11-year cycle of sunspot activity, but intense solar flares can produce spectacular auroral displays at any time during the cycle. These brilliant illuminations are also present in skies far from Earth: future space travelers can look forward to enjoying the auroras that have now been documented on Jupiter, Saturn, Mars, Uranus, Venus and Neptune, as well on three of Jupiter's moons: Io, Europa and Ganymede. ∎

Shimmering *The aurora borealis appears in its most common "curtain" form above a home in Kautokeino in northern Norway*

Auroras: The Basics

Q. What are auroras?
A. They are illuminations in the sky produced by the reaction of the solar wind's ionized gases with Earth's magnetic field, the magnetosphere.

Q. Why are auroras mainly a polar phenomenon?
A. The magnetic poles at either end of the planet create electro-magnetic "funnels" that attract the charged particles of the solar wind.

Q. When do auroras peak?
A. They are most prominent at the apex of the sun's 11-year sunspot cycle, next due in late 2011 or early 2012. They are also more prominent near the planet's two yearly equinoxes, for reasons not yet clear to scientists.

Q. What does the term aurora borealis mean?
A. Aurora is the goddess of the dawn in Greek mythology. Boreas was the ancient Greeks' name for the north wind.

the auroras at the North and South Poles are not mirror images of each other

Voyagers

O N DEC. 25, 1758, A VISITOR FROM THE HEAVENS brought great tidings to Earth. That Christmas night, Johann Georg Palitzsch, a German farmer and amateur astronomer, noted a tiny smudge of light in the sky. This vision was the first proof of one of the most hotly debated scientific theories of the time: noted British astronomer Edmond Halley's prediction that the comets referred to in histories of the years 1682 and 1531—as well as the comet viewed by the famed pioneer astronomer Johannes Kepler in 1607— were all observations of the same heavenly body, which was visible from Earth every 75 years or so as it orbited the sun. Halley's estimate that the comet would return in 1758 was thus proved true in the last week of the year. Sadly, the scientist died in 1742, too early to see his prophecy fulfilled.

Early humans believed comets were portents that presaged historic events. As outlaws in the sky that do not follow the familiar patterns of the stars and planets, comets and their long, wispy tails have long been of special interest to astronomers. At one time they were believed to resemble aggregates of ice pebbles akin to flying shoals of gravel. In the mid-20th century, U.S. astronomer Fred Whipple proposed that comets were conglomerates of ice and dust, and flybys of Halley's last appearance in 1986 and of Comet Borrelly in 2001 confirmed that those comets indeed resembled "dirty snowballs." However, data from Borrelly also showed that it has a hot, dry surface, so scientists remain uncertain as to the amount of ice present within any given comet.

Scientists enjoyed their closest encounter with a comet in 2005, thanks to NASA's Deep Impact mission, in which a spacecraft sent a probe crashing to the surface of Comet 9P/Tempel. The probe successfully excavated debris from the comet's nucleus, which photos indicated was less dusty and held more ice than predicted, unlike Borelly. The debris was also finer than expected, more like talcum powder than sand.

A comet's signature tail is created by the same force that shapes auroras: the solar wind, made up of charged particles released by the sun, excites the ice and dust in a comet. These charged elements are in turn released in the glowing arcs of the tails, which sometimes are clearly seen to be twins, one of gas and one of dust, which always point away from the sun. ■

Just Passing Through

Above, Comet Hale-Bopp lights up the sky in Gotha, Germany, on April 2, 1997, almost two years after it was discovered independently by Alan Hale in New Mexico and Thomas Bopp in Arizona on July 23, 1995. Hale-Bopp put on the most prominent display of any comet in recent decades, first becoming visible to the naked eye in May 1996, then fading from view as it grew closer to the sun. It reappeared in much brighter form in January 1997, and its visibility peaked in February 1997. Scientists found that in addition to gas and dust tails, Hale-Bopp had a smaller tail of sodium.

Data Stream: Most comets originate in two regions on the outskirts of the solar system, the Kuiper Belt and

Four Recent Comets

Astronomers classify comets into two main groups. Those that orbit the sun within a span of 200 years are called periodic comets; those with longer solar orbits are non-periodic. "Great comets" are those that can be seen with the naked eye.

Hale-Bopp Dubbed the "Great Comet of 1997," this visitor was far brighter than Halley's Comet was in its 1986 appearance and was easily visible to the naked eye. Return: 4377.

Halley's The 1986 flyby of the best-known comet was one of its weaker appearances, far less bright than its 1910 visit. Return: 2061.

McNaught This most recent "great comet" was first sighted in August 2006 and made its closest approach to Earth early in 2007. Scientists are uncertain when, if ever, it will return.

Shoemaker-Levy 9 This comet split into 20-some pieces as it drew near Jupiter, then slammed into the planet over a six-day period in 1994, in what has been called the most violent event ever seen from Earth.

Celestial Tattoos

EACH DAY SOME 1.4 MILLION METEOROIDS, CAP-
tives of gravity, pass into Earth's atmosphere.
The vast majority of them are smallish objects
that heat up and disintegrate as they encounter the
planet's invisible barrier of air. Some, like those we see
during the annual Leonid and Perseid meteor showers,
are the predictable result of the planet's rendezvous
with meteoroid clusters also in orbit around the sun.
Most are tiny, unexpected visitors that die memorably,
leaving fiery scrawls of sparks across the sky. And a
very few of them are of such an enormous size as to
change the course of history.

One such impact with an asteroid estimated to be 6
miles in diameter took place in the region of Chicxulub
on Mexico's Yucatán Peninsula some 65 million years
ago. That event is now believed by many scientists to
have sent so much debris into the planet's skies that
much of Earth's vegetation died off, resulting in the
extinction of the dinosaurs. Yet meteoroids may also be
life givers; some scientists believe life may first have trav-
eled to Earth in the form of bacteria carried on them.

The terminology of these heavenly bodies is precise:
astronomers draw a distinction between meteoroids,
which are small objects drifting in outer space;
meteors, which are meteoroids that have entered the
planet's atmosphere and are often visible as "shooting
stars"; and meteorites, the term used to describe a
meteor once it has landed on Earth. One such unexpected arrival took place in Freehold Township, N.J.,
on Jan. 2, 2007, when a meteor crashed through the
roof of a home, bounced off a tile floor and came to rest
embedded in a wall, now a meteorite. Roughly the size
of a golfball, the object weighed a bit less than a pound.
Fortunately, no humans or dinosaurs were injured. ■

JEAN PAUL FERRERO—AUSCAPE—MINDEN PICTURES

Too-Close Encounters

Three impact craters—at top, Wolfe Creek in Australia; above left, Barringer Crater in Arizona; above right, Gosses Bluff in Australia—offer dramatic evidence of the result of collisions between Earth and large celestial objects. The possibility of such collisions is now of consuming interest to scientists, especially since the 21-part Shoemaker-Levy 9 comet smashed into Jupiter in 1994 with a force far greater than that of all the nuclear weapons now existing combined. Asteroids and comets whose orbit brings them dangerously close to the planet are known as near Earth objects, and the orbits of the 800 largest of them are closely monitored.

Ten Major Impact Craters

Some sites of asteroid impact, like the Wolfe Creek crater in Australia at left, are well known and of a size easily grasped; others are so vast and ancient that they are best traced from space or an airplane. The Geology.com website offers an interactive Google map that displays pictures of each crater below.

Aorounga, Chad
Age (est.): 2-300 million years
Diameter: 10.5 miles (17 km)

Barringer Crater, U.S.
Age (est.): 49,000 years
Diameter: 0.74 miles (1.2 km)

Bosumtwi, Ghana
Age (est.): 1.3 million years
Diameter: 6.5 miles (10.5 km)

Chicxulub, Mexico
Age (est.): 65 million years
Diameter: 105 miles (170 km)
Note: this is the impact now believed to have led to the extinction of the dinosaurs

Clearwater Lakes, Canada
Age (est.): 290 million years
Diameter, West: 20 miles (32 km)
Diameter, East: 13.7 miles (22 km)
Note: these twin craters were created by a pair of asteroids

Deep Bay, Canada
Age (est.): 100 million years
Diameter: 8 miles (13 km)

Gosses Bluff, Australia
Age (est.): 142 million years
Diameter: 15 miles (24 km)

Kara-Kul, Tajikistan
Age (est.): 5 million years
Diameter: 28 miles (45 km)

Manicouagan, Canada
Age (est.): 212 million years
Diameter: 62 miles (100 km)

Mistastin Lake, Canada
Age (est.): 38 million years
Diameter: 17.4 miles (28 km)

Source: Solarviews.com

13

Collision Course?

"THAT ONE WOULD HAVE PUNCHED RIGHT THROUGH the atmosphere with no trouble," Donald Yeomans told TIME early in 2008. Yeomans is the director of NASA's Near Earth Objects (NEO) program, which means he's in charge of hunting comets and asteroids whose solar orbits put them on a potential collision course with our planet. He is referring to 2007 TU24, a 750-ft. (229 m) -long chunk of rock that went whizzing past our world on Jan. 29, 2008, going 6 miles per second—yes, that's 21,600 m.p.h.

Spotted the previous October, TU24 was listed by NASA as a "current impact risk" until just over a month before it flew by. If it hadn't missed us, Yeomans estimates, the asteroid would have survived Earth's only line of defense—the atmosphere, which burns up all but the largest objects inbound from space—and would have detonated with an explosive force equivalent to 100,000 Hiroshima-sized atom bombs. Such a blast over land could erase an area the size of New England. If it hit the ocean, its impact would have sent massive tsunamis radiating in every direction.

"Hundreds of tons of interplanetary material rain down on the Earth every day," Yeomans says. "Most of these are very small particles, but we get objects the size of a basketball every 24 hours or so, and something the size of a Volkswagen roughly once a week." All of them are incinerated by the atmosphere. But any asteroid with a diameter of more than 460 ft. (140 m) is likely to penetrate our protective blanket of air and cause serious damage on the ground. "That size would cause a regionally destructive event," he says. "Objects in the range of 1,000 ft. (304 m) across would devastate entire countries. Anything more than 1 km in diameter would cause worldwide problems."

Not so long ago, nobody was looking for killer space rocks. "In the early 1990s, our biggest problem was the 'giggle factor,'" Yeomans says. "People assumed we were nutty scientists or else interpreted [our concerns] as a cynical scare tactic to get our research funded. But in 1998, two not very good movies about objects from space potentially devastating the planet—*Deep Impact* and *Armageddon*—were big hits, and suddenly the public and elected officials were willing to take the threat seriously. That was the year Congress finally agreed to budget money for the NEO program."

Since 1998, Yeomans and his team have been systematically scanning the skies for "asteroids that have Earth's name on them." So far, they have identified 948 "Potentially Hazardous Asteroids," space rocks close enough to slam into Earth and large enough to penetrate the atmosphere. That's about 90% of the biggest global threats, they believe. They're now turning to the second phase of their search: compiling a catalog of the far more numerous asteroids that could cause regional or national devastation. More than 50 of those big enough make the regionally destructive cut are expected to make close approaches to Earth in 2008 alone, and fully half of these were spotted for the first time in the past five years. "We're going around the sun in a swarm of near Earth objects, many of which could hit us," Yeomans observes.

But what's the point in spotting incoming artillery if you can't do anything about? "Actually, there's quite a lot we could do about it," Yeomans says. He points to the statistical likelihood that an incoming asteroid large enough to cause widespread destruction would be spotted as long as decades in advance. "We think we've found most of the very large asteroids," he says, "and we're now tracing their movements into the future. So almost certainly, if one of these is going to hit Earth, we'll know 20 to 40 years in advance."

Given that amount of notice, Yeomans says, existing technology could give the asteroid a slight nudge, just enough to speed it up or slow it down slightly. "Over the vast distances and lengths of time we're talking about," he explains, "this would be enough to ensure that the asteroid crossed the path of Earth's orbit either too early or too late, and simply miss us."

This gentle shove could be achieved in a number of ways. "A rocket engine the size of the one on the space shuttle would be more than big enough," Yeomans says. "Or a lens to concentrate incoming solar energy could be used to boil off part of the surface and create a jet effect. It might even be possible to attach a solar sail to the object, a large membrane that would be 'pushed' by solar radiation the way a canvas sail is by wind." One nonstarter as a tactic, he says, is "the Bruce Willis approach. You wouldn't want to blow up a large asteroid, because then you'd have a shotgun blast of incoming debris, rather than a single bullet."

Asked if he worries his labors may be in vain, he notes that large asteroids have gouged out more than 300 impact craters worldwide, with many more likely still undiscovered or made unrecognizable by the passage of time. "More impacts are coming," he declares. "It's a question of when, not if." ■

Burnout *A meteor shower paints streaks in the sky over Joshua Tree National Park in California. Unlike the "killer" NEOs tracked by NASA, the objects in such annual meteor showers as the Perseids and the Leonids are too small to pass through the atmospheric barrier intact and damage the planet*

Breath of the Gods

THE WIND GOETH TOWARD THE SOUTH, AND TURN-eth about unto the north," the Old Testament's Book of Ecclesiastes reports. "It whirleth about continually, and the wind returneth again according to his circuits." This forecast is still accurate, but what exactly, uh, driveth the wind, one of nature's most essential, if unseen, forces? The circulation of air is powered by the same source from which all earthly energy comes, either directly or indirectly: the sun.

As the sun's warming rays fall upon the earth, the air doesn't toast evenly: the equator receives more direct, concentrated rays than do the poles, so temperatures around the equatorial belt are higher. This mass of warmer air responds by expanding and floating upward. Since the expanding air is thinner than the surrounding atmosphere, as it rises, there's less of it near the ground, causing a local drop in air pressure. Because nature abhors a vacuum, nearby masses of cooler, denser air (which is necessarily under higher pressure) rush in to fill the empty spaces.

This movement of air is the wind. Its direction is determined by the relative positions of the high and low pressure zones, and its speed is a function of the difference in pressures. Although the temperature gap between the equator and the poles is one of the primary drivers of our planet's wind, there are others: land and water absorb and hold the sun's heat at different rates, as do various kinds of terra firma. All of these asymmetries lead to local differences in air temperature, which are registered in the behavior of the wind.

The wind helps shape life on the earth and even shapes the planet itself: moving air ferries particles of sand and soil, as well as seeds, across vast distances (sometimes over entire oceans and continents), carries both the water (in the form of vapor) that gives life and the microbes that sometimes take it away, causes clouds (and most other weather-related phenomenon) to form and actually sculpts the ground, eroding solid rock over thousands of years. So familiar is the wind that local gusts have been christened with their own names, from A to Z: the Abroholos is a summer squall off the coast of Brazil, while Zephyr is the ancient Greek name for the West Wind.

Winds can even speed up and slow down the planet's rotation. El Niño storms and other strong winds that blow counter to the planet's spin can exert enough frictional drag on its surface to produce a small but measurable decrease in its speed of rotation, thus

RIGHT: MICHA PAWLITZKI—ZEFA—CORBIS

Shooting the breeze *The wind is invisible, but these three pictures capture its power. At far left, a cypress tree on the Caribbean island of Barbados has been contorted into a permanently twisted shape by steady breezes. At near left, winds have eroded the outer layers of chalk deposits to shape these odd globular forms in Egypt's White Desert, the Sahara el Beyda. Below, a strong gust of wind has moved a rock across the dry bed of the Death Valley desert in the U.S., leaving behind a clear trail of its movement*

lengthening each day ever so slightly. Winters with strong westerly winds in the northern hemisphere (which puff in tandem with the earth's spin) produce a minute increase in the world's twirl, thus shortening each day by a few thousandths of a second.

The whirling globe, in turn, can drive the winds: the Coriolis force created by the earth's spin makes prevailing winds blow from west to east in the northern hemisphere and from east to west in the southern. It also causes hurricanes to spin counterclockwise above the equator and clockwise below.

Much of our knowledge of the wind is recent. Jet streams, the ribbons of high-altitude wind that gust around the globe at speeds of up to 250 m.p.h. (400 km/h), were first observed by amateur meteorologist Clement Ley in the 1880s and were not actually encountered until the 1930s, when pioneering aviator Wiley Post took a small plane up to 40,000 ft. (12 km) and found himself clipping along at twice the speed his engine could produce. Yet these streams play a key role in shaping the planet's climate. The more we learn about this potent but invisible force, the more the ancient Greeks seem to have had the right description for it: wind, they claimed, is the breath of the gods. ■

Forecast: Grit Showers

THE ARABIC WORDS FOR "WIND" AND "PHENOME-non" merge to form the term haboob, which scientists use to describe the enormous sand and dust storms that are a regular feature of life in desert climes. Although haboobs form primarily in a broad swath of arid land stretching from northern Africa across the Arabian Peninsula to Iraq and Iran, they are known to occur in other places in the world, including the arid desert regions of the Southwestern U.S.

Haboobs can be thought of as dry monsoons that pelt the ground with particulate matter instead of rain. They generally form when the low-pressure conditions that create thunderstorms collapse. As cold air from high altitudes rushes into the former area of low pressure, it first thrusts toward the ground, then is deflected outward. The resulting winds may pick up as much as several hundred tons of loose desert debris. The unforgettable result is a giant brown or black wall of violently churning grime, most often 1,000 to 3,000 ft. high and as much as 60 miles wide, whose winds

Special Delivery from Africa

Haboobs can be so enormous as to straddle continents: in extreme cases, sand kicked up by North African haboobs can be deposited as a film of talcum-like dirt on cars in southern Europe. In the satellite image above, sand from the Sahara Desert is moving north across Egypt and crossing the Mediterranean Sea to reach Europe. The Nile delta is visible as a triangle of green to the right of the sandstorm. Scientists are only beginning to probe the role played by sandstorms in moving minerals and seeds around the globe.

Sandstorms in an Oasis City

Motorists drive through a sandstorm in Turfan (Turpan), an oasis city in northwest China that is surrounded by arid plains and receives less than 1 in. of rainfall a year. The nearby Turfan Depression, a trough created at the border of two tectonic plates, makes Turfan one of the world's lowest-lying cities. An ancient system of wells and canals brings water into the city, making it habitable for humans.

churn suspended particulates at up to 60 m.p.h.

In this picture, a haboob bearing sand and dust from the Sahara Desert rolls into Khartoum, Sudan's capital. Residents of the Middle East are so familiar with such storms that they have given them specific names. The season's first storm, which usually arrives in the last week of May, is called al-Haffar, or "the Driller," because it scrapes huge holes in desert sand dunes. The next, which most often comes in early June, is called Barih Thorayya, since it arrives with the dawn star, Thorayya. The last storm of the season is called al-Dabaran, "the Follower"; it's infamous for carrying a particularly penetrating layer of microscopic dust that finds its way into seemingly every crevice and corner in its path. ■

The Thunderbolt

THE GREEKS CALLED LIGHTNING THE "THUNDER-bolt" and depicted it as a jagged line of energy hurled by Zeus to dazzle and intimidate human beings. And there was some truth embedded in the myth, for though lightning is one of nature's most thrilling and brilliant phenomena, for centuries it was deeply feared as a fire starter in lands where most buildings were constructed of highly combustible wood. The problem plagued mankind until the 18th century, when Benjamin Franklin's lightning rod tamed the terror from the sky, as discussed at right.

There's plenty of room for a new Franklin in the field of lightning studies, for scientists still don't completely understand its complex mechanisms. We know, for example, that most lightning begins when clouds acquire an electrical charge, or become ionized, with the upper portion usually positive and the bottom portion most often negative. But we still don't understand in full the forces that drive the charging of the air. On one point there's no doubt, however: this ionized air is highly conductive and provides the pathway for lightning to flow to earth.

A strike occurs when an ionized column of air connects two areas with opposite charges, which are always attracted to each other. As the ionized air extends its force outward in the form of negatively charged "stepped leaders," the earth responds to this strong electrical field by sending "positive streamers" upward. When a stepped leader meets a positive streamer, a current flows between cloud and earth in the form of plasma, discharging energy in a familiar one-two punch: FLASH! … BOOM! The thunderbolt's exchange of energy produces high heat—that's the lightning flash. The explosion also creates a shockwave we hear as a sonic boom— and that's the thunder. The delay betwen the two is science anyone can understand: everyday proof that light travels far faster than sound. ∎

Nature's Fireworks

Lightning strikes are more common around the globe in regions where both temperatures and humidity levels are high. For those reasons, lands near the equator tend to experience the most electrical storms. The most lightning-prone region on the planet is in the Democratic Republic of Congo. At left, lightning bolts touch ground at Ayers Rock/Uluru in the Australian outback, one of the planet's most striking geological formations; above is a twin strike in Rio de Janeiro. In the U.S., the region that experiences the highest number of lightning strikes each year is central Florida, where afternoon thunderstorms are almost a daily occurrence.

From the dawn of history, lightning has been one of the great scourges of mankind, touching off deadly fires. It was not until the 18th century, when scientists and educated laymen like Benjamin Franklin began delving into the secrets of electricity, that the threat of fire from lightning was finally reduced. Franklin was one of the first to propose that lightning strikes were a form of electricity and could be diverted safely into the ground by the use of metal rods mounted on rooftops. This theory, controversial and even the subject of mockery when first advanced, was proved correct by French scientists on May 10, 1752—making Franklin celebrated around the world as a benefactor of mankind.

Altitude with Attitude

WATER IS ONE OF NATURE'S SHAPE SHIFTERS, familiar in its liquid and frozen forms. Yet it's easy to forget that the clouds over our heads also are carriers of water, in this case in its vapor form. Clouds are one of nature's everyday wonders, hiding in plain sight until they are touched with the sun's reflected glory at sunrise and sunset or pile up to form a lightning-generating, anvil-headed cumulonimbus thundercloud or simply release their moisture in the form of rain or snow.

Scientists divide clouds into two main categories: stratus clouds, which form a horizontal plane in the sky, and cumulus clouds, the puffy ones with cotton-candy shapes. And everyone is familiar with the types of clouds that are generated in different levels of the atmosphere: wispy, high-flying cirrus clouds that reach into the troposphere, 20,000 ft. (6,000 m) above the planet; the towering middle-level clouds, identified by the prefix *alto-* (e.g., altostratus, altocumulus) that range from 6,500 to 20,000 ft. (2,000 to 6,000 m) above our heads; and the low clouds (including stratus and cumulus) that hover around 6,500 ft. (2,000 m). When clouds come in for a landing with the ground, we call them fog. Each of the categories above is further subdivided into classifications and combinations that are of interest primarily to nephologists—an old-fashioned word for meteorologists who study clouds.

Since clouds are creatures of the wind, they can

Proud clouds *A trio of splendid cloud formations: on this page, a shelf cloud above Clearwater, Fla; at right, lenticular clouds atop the Himalayas and the Andes. While some areas across the globe experience regular cloud patterns, only a few unusual cloud formations recur frequently. The best known is perhaps the "Morning Glory" cloud, a tube-shaped cloud that can be 600 miles (1,000 km) long; similar to a shelf cloud, it accompanies severe weather formations in northern Australia's Gulf of Carpentaria*

assume some fascinating shapes. The main picture above shows a shelf cloud dominating the sky above Clearwater, Fla. A shelf cloud's very distinct edge typically delineates the limit of a weather front. In this case, the cloud is the leading edge of a tropical thunderstorm moving above the coastline.

The smaller pictures are examples of lenticular clouds, lens-shaped formations generally found at high altitudes and often shaped by the flow of wind over a mountain range. The top picture shows an unusual diamond-shaped lenticular formation above Mount Everest. The bottom picture shows a tall lenticular cloud that formed above the Fitzroy Massif in Los Glaciares National Park, Argentina. ∎

Storm Clouds: A Glossary

Cumulonimbus These classic, dark thunderstorm-brewing clouds have the tall, puffy shape of cumulus clouds but carry far more moisture. Their strong up-drafts elevate warm, unstable rising air to their anvil-shaped tops, where the water can freeze into hail.

Mammatus Derived from the Latin word for breast, this term describes clouds that form a honeycomb of low-hanging pouches; they often precede a storm.

Supercell The most severe class of thunderstorm clouds, these form around a continuously rotating updraft that can become a tornado.

Tornadic This adjectival, increasingly familiar form of the word *tornado* describes the swiftly rotating storm clouds that coalesce to form a funnel reaching to the ground at the onset of a twister.

Arc of light *The sky is clearing, but enough water is suspended in the atmosphere to form a rainbow in New Mexico*

Spectacular Spectrums

MOST OF US WOULD HEARTILY AGREE WITH William Wordsworth: "My heart leaps up when I behold/ A rainbow in the sky." It's difficult not to be dazzled by this evanescent visual phenomenon, which the Old Testament describes as a sign of God's covenant with Noah after the flood. The fascination of this offspring of sunlight and raindrops never dims: the hipsters of British rock group Radiohead titled their 2007 hit album *In Rainbows*.

If you've seen a rainbow, you know its power to thrill. So let's skip the poetry and move to the prosaic: What is it, exactly, we're beholding when our heart makes that familiar leap? Rainbows are only the most common form of a number of fascinating visual phenomena that adorn the planet, some so fragile that they simply can't be photographed.

Rainbows are formed by the interplay between water and light. When white sunlight moves through a water droplet, it is refracted, or bent, and splits into the seven visible colors that compose it: from the outside in, that's red, orange, yellow, green, blue, indigo and violet (or "Roy G. Biv," the mnemonic chap well known to schoolkids). Why? Because each of those colors operates on its own distinct wavelength. In this case, raindrops are acting like the prisms through which Isaac Newton passed light and separated it in his pioneering work on the science of optics.

There's more to rainbows than meets the eye: the light spectrum actually forms a round rainbow in the sky, but our view of it is limited by the horizon, so a rainbow appears as a semicircle. But from an airplane, it's possible to see Mr. Biv as a complete circle.

Rainbows are elusive phenomena, but if you've seen a moonbow: congratulations. This much less common optical phenomenon occurs when moonlight passes through raindrops or water vapor and forms a circular spectrum. Moonbows are generally only seen on clear nights when the moon is full; certain of the world's waterfalls, like Africa's Victoria Falls and Lower Yosemite Falls in California, right, are noted for the frequency with which moonbows appear.

Sundogs are another of nature's fascinating optical phenomena. Scientists call them parhelions; they most often form when the sun is low in a sky filled with ice crystals within cirrus clouds. The effect varies: sometimes two false suns appear on either side of the star; at other times a full halo is visible; sometimes the visual effect more resembles a stained smudge of light with a tail than it does a false sun. In all cases, your eyes aren't playing tricks on you; nature is. ■

Visions *A parhelion (sundog) with a halo and two false suns forms as ice crystals refract sunlight in the Nunavut territory in northern Canada*

Full-moon fever *A faint moonbow shimmers over Lower Yosemite Falls*

In Harm's Way

THE GOOD NEWS: THE ALARMING VISION ON THESE pages does not show a trio of three massive hurricanes heading across Florida and the U.S. Gulf Coast at once; this view from a NASA weather satellite is a composite image that shows the position of Hurricane Andrew as it moved from east to west (right to left) across the Florida peninsula and the Gulf Coast, on the days of Aug. 23, 24 and 25, 1992.

Andrew was one of the most devastating hurricanes in U.S. history. The Category 5 storm unleashed steady winds with speeds up to 155 m.p.h. (250 km/h), with occasional gusts of much higher speed. The big blow claimed 65 lives and caused more than $38 billion in damage (in 2008 dollars). In the years since 1992, hurricane activity has risen dramatically along the Gulf Coast. A quartet of hurricanes pummeled the region in 2004, and 2005's Hurricane Katrina was the worst natural disaster to strike a major U.S. city since the San Francisco earthquake and fire of 1906.

Demonstrating the complex relationships that drive

Earth's weather events, most of the big storms that plague the U.S. East Coast are spawned in Africa. Most Atlantic hurricanes originate in "easterly waves," disturbances in barometric pressure and wind speed caused when extreme heat from the Sahara Desert in north Africa butts up against cooler temperatures along the Gulf of Guinea on the west African coast.

As an easterly wave moves west across the Atlantic, it develops into a hurricane in a four-part process. The wave, which meteorologists call a tropical disturbance, becomes a tropical depression when its winds reach speeds of up to 38 m.p.h. (61 km/h) and begin to rotate around a central vortex. The depression becomes a tropical storm when wind speeds increase to 39 to 73 m.p.h. (63 to 117 km/h) and the central vortex becomes more delineated. The final hurricane stage is reached when winds exceed 74 m.p.h. (119 km/h). Hurricane Andrew's peak gusts in southern Florida were not recorded: the storm destroyed all official measuring equipment on the ground. ■

Twisters in Transition

TORNADOES ARE AMONG NATURE'S MOST UNPRE-
dictable events: once a twister drops down from
a supercell cloud and starts raising a ruckus, it's
very difficult to anticipate the exact path it will follow.
But for many decades, these frightening storms at least
followed certain patterns: they were usually confined
to a sector of the nation's midsection dubbed Tornado
Alley, which runs from Oklahoma through Kansas and
Missouri and east to Illinois, Indiana, Ohio, Tennessee
and Kentucky. And they appeared during an annual
tornado season: Midwesterners scouted the skies for
twisters from spring into the first weeks of summer.

Of course, as the National Oceanographic and Atmospheric Agency (NOAA) reminds visitors to its website,
in italics for emphasis: *Violent or killer tornadoes do
happen outside Tornado Alley every year.* And *Tornadoes
can happen any time of year.* But until recently, these
warnings seemed pro forma, an acknowledgment that
even Uncle Sam can't predict the weather. But consider
the events of March 14, 2008, in downtown Atlanta.
While 18,000 fans filled the Georgia Dome for the
Southeastern Conference basketball tournament and
16,107 NBA fans jammed Philips Arena for a game
between the hometown Hawks and the Los Angeles
Clippers, a twister cut a six-mile (10 km) path of ruin
through the city's heart. Winds gusted up to 130 m.p.h.
(209 km/h), crushing homes, ripping façades off buildings, downing trees and shattering glass. Authorities in

both buildings chose not to alert fans to the severe
weather outside, even as tiles fell from the ceiling
and catwalks swayed in the Georgia Dome.

When the Weather Channel's version of March
Madness ended, some 27 people had been injured
in the first tornado ever to strike in the downtown
of Georgia's capital city, and officials estimated the
damage at $250 million. The next day, smaller twisters
claimed two lives in areas of rural Georgia.

Tornadoes are also jumping the tracks of their
predictable seasons these days. Over the four days
from Jan. 7 to 11, 2008—in the depths of winter, never
regarded as a twister-breeding period—a barrage of
72 separate tornadoes roared through areas around
the Mississippi Valley, ranging from southwestern
Missouri and northwestern Arkansas to Alabama and
Mississippi; four people were killed. Less than a month
later, on Feb. 5-6, a staggering 82 confirmed tornadoes
touched down in Tennessee, Arkansas and the southern
Ohio Valley, killing 58 people in four states. It was the
deadliest tornado assault in the U.S. since 1985.

What's going on? Meteorologists fear that climate
change driven by global warming is brewing up a new
generation of tornadoes that will strike more frequently,
with greater severity and over a broader swath of the
country than before. Their advice: prepare today, for
Tornado Alley is now Tornado Superhighway, and
twisters are now storms for all seasons. ∎

Spinning mayhem *Tornadoes are most often spawned by supercell storms, like the one shown at left, whirling above Nebraska on May 28, 2004. Supercells are severe thunderstorms that form around a deep, constantly rotating updraft called a mesocyclone. The updraft tilts the inflowing air into a vertical position and sets its spinning. Often, through a process not yet completely understood, an even more rapidly spinning funnel drops to the ground: a tornado. That's what happened in Pampa, Texas, in 1995, forming the big twister on this page. The air pressure inside a tornado is much lower than the pressure outside it, creating a vortex that "inhales" anything around it*

hydr●sphere

hy·dro·sphere *(n.)*
[Gk *hydror* water + Gk *sphaira* ball]
all the waters on the earth's surface, such as oceans, rivers,
lakes and seas; the world of water

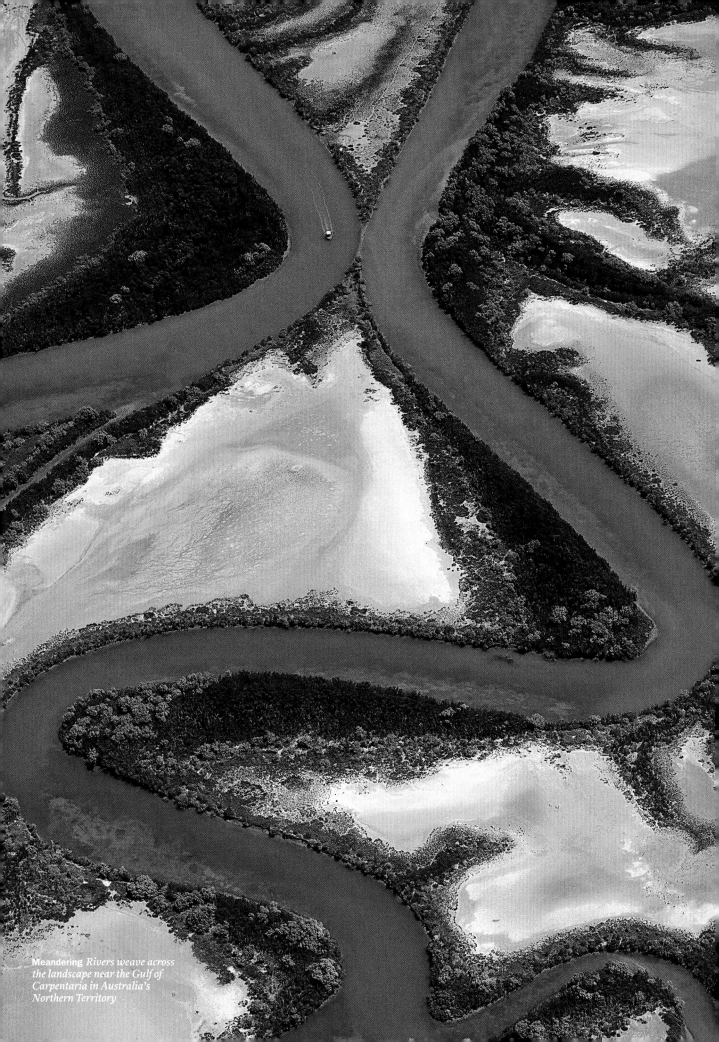

Meandering *Rivers weave across the landscape near the Gulf of Carpentaria in Australia's Northern Territory*

Abode of the Clouds

WHAT'S THE SINGLE RAINIEST PLACE ON THE planet? According to British travel writer Alexander Frater's delightful 1990 book *Chasing the Monsoon* (Alfred A. Knopf), the distinction goes to the northeast Indian city of Cherrapunji. But two other contenders are often said to be even wetter: Mount Waialeale in Hawaii and Cherrapunji's sister city in the Indian state of Meghalaya, Mawsynram.

The battle for this moist accolade involves so much volleying of statistics that it may be of interest only to meteorologists—and the boosterish residents of the three drenched domains. But here are some facts to consider. Cherrapunji holds the record for having experienced the single rainiest month ever recorded: in July 1861, 366 in. (9.3 m) fell from the heavens. (Yes, that's more than 30 ft., or 3.7 m, of rainfall in one

month). The 12-month record was also set here in the same *annus pouribilis*, when 1,041 in. (26.4 m) was recorded. Today Cherrapunji's annual rainfall is 428 in. (11.43 m). Down the road in Mawsynram, the average is a tad higher, at 467 in. (11.8 m). And over on the Hawaiian island of Kauai, the average rainfall on Mount Waialeale is 460 in. (11.6 m). But watch out, Mawsynram: according to scientists from the University of Krakow in Poland, annual rainfall in Cherrapunji has been increasing for the past 30 years or so.

We've split the difference between Cherrapunji and Mawsynram in the picture above, which shows Khasi farmers tending their crops during the monsoon season outside Shillong, the capital city of Meghalaya, which means "the Abode of the Clouds." Both Cherrapunji and Mawsynram lie close to Shillong in the

heights of the Khasi Hills, just north of Bangladesh, which is buffeted by extreme monsoon rains every year from June until September. The Khasis are one of three ancient and distinct ethnic groups that dwell in Meghalaya; the others are the Jaintias and the Garos. Adequate rain gear is one of life's essentials here: the Khasi farmers above are wearing traditional *knups*, woven bamboo hats/umbrellas/raincoats that cover not only their heads but most of their bodies.

Whether you wear a *knup* every day or only unfurl an umbrella now and then, the planet's rain cycle makes your life possible. The transfer of water in all its forms is one of the most complex, if familiar, processes on the earth. Scientists call it the hydrologic cycle. The system is powered by solar heat, which evaporates water from the planet's oceans, rivers and lakes. The

water vapor that results is borne by the wind long distances around the globe, until local weather conditions cause it to condense into clouds, then to fall back to the surface as rain, snow or other precipitation.

Rainwater that falls on a body of water is quickly absorbed. Some of the rain that falls on the land infiltrates the ground, eventually ending up in the water table. Some is absorbed by plants and trees and then released back into the atmosphere as water vapor in the process called transpiration. When rain falls on a land surface that is too hard to absorb the water, it flows over the ground until it joins a river or stream, in a process called runoff. That is the case in Cherrapunji, where the local limestone bedrock doesn't absorb water well, and retention facilities are inadequate: one of Earth's rainiest towns suffers water shortages each year. ∎

When the Rains Reign

THE GREAT MONSOON RAINS THAT DRENCH INDIA and much of southern Asia every year from June through September are one of the largest and most reliable of the planet's annual weather patterns. The rains are an indelible fact of life there, shaping agriculture, commerce and customs. Like the annual floods along the Nile in Egypt, the monsoons help irrigate fields that would otherwise be fallow. The yearly arrival of the rains is much awaited, an occasion for festivities celebrating seasonal renewal.

A weather pattern of such intensity and regularity is driven by many distinct engines. Wind patterns, water temperatures and other factors play important roles in shaping each year's monsoon season. But a 2008 report published in *Nature* magazine found an unexpected, longer-term influence: the length and intensity of monsoon seasons, it claimed, are affected by tiny wobbles in the planet's orbit as it revolves around the sun. Monsoon seasons wax and wane in a 23,000-year pattern that reflects the rhythm of these orbital irregularities, the researchers declared, reflecting differences in levels of solar radiation due to the slight orbital fluctuations.

Where does one go to measure the effects of an orbital wobble? The team of researchers from Nanjing Normal University in China headed underground,

Long commute *The town of Kishoreganj in Bangladesh is cut off from the mainland for six months every year during the monsoon flood season, and residents use a bamboo bridge to get around*

studying stalagmites from a cave in eastern China to measure changes in climate patterns over the past quarter-million years. Their conclusion: we are living through a period of moderate monsoons compared with those of recent millenniums.

Scientists are alarmed about the effect of rising temperatures on the monsoons. A 2006 study found that global warming is making the annual rains more intense as ocean water heats up; even more alarming, it found that warming may disrupt the steady calendar of the deluges. Considering the billions of humans who live off crops nourished by the rains, a year without monsoons could be a global catastrophe. ■

Monsoons: The Basics

Q. What are they?
A. These heavy, localized seasonal rains are caused when air over the land rises in temperature, creating low-pressure zones that attract moist ocean air in the form of rain clouds.

Q. Where do they occur?
A. The largest annual monsoon rains occur on the Asian subcontinent, but life in sub-Saharan Africa is also dominated by seasonal monsoons. Australia, East Asia and some locales in the Americas experience less severe monsoons than South Asia.

Lion king *A Galápagos sea lion is outnumbered by a school of salemas at a depth of about 30 ft. (9 m) off Ecuador's Galápagos Islands*

The Water Planet

THOSE WHO HAVE SEEN PLANET EARTH FROM OUTER SPACE OFTEN COMPARE IT TO A BLUE MARBLE suspended in front of the stars. It's the oceans that put the blue in that blue marble, for ours is a water planet, 71% of whose surface is covered by saline seas. Indeed, though we have given names to five specific oceans—the Pacific, Atlantic, Indian, Arctic and Southern—there is in fact only one great ocean on the planet, and it encircles all the world's continents. In these vast waters, most scientists believe, life forms first emerged on the planet. Water remains a critical component in almost every form of life on Earth, and the fluid chemistry of the human body is remarkably similar to that of seawater: in a sense, the oceans are not only all around us but inside us as well.

The oceans are key drivers of the earth's climate, taking in solar energy that warms their waters, then distributing the heat around the globe in the process called surface circulation. Influenced by the Coriolis effect, created by the planet's spin, surface circulation operates through a series of circular gyres that carry warm water away from the equator and cold water toward it. The Gulf Stream and Japan Current are familiar examples of prevailing surface-circulation currents; it is the hot water borne by the Japan Current that creates the temperate, rainy climate of the U.S.'s Pacific Northwest. Deeper ocean currents move more slowly, in a process called thermohaline circulation.

Interacting with the atmosphere, the oceans also play a major role in the irrigation of the planet, as solar heat evaporates seawater and carries it into the atmosphere, where it forms rain clouds. And the oceans are also vast reservoirs of life, filled with plants and animals that help feed the planet, including the billions of humans who rely on the sea for sustenance. Biologists estimate that some 250,000 distinct species of animals live in the ocean, with more discovered every year. Yet even though the oceans are the foundation of life on Earth, they are relatively unexplored. Their depths were alien territory until the latter part of the 20th century, and scientists today know more about the surfaces of the moon and Mars than they do about the seabeds under the oceans. The water planet promises to be a fascinating new frontier for scientific exploration in the 21st century. ■

Land, Earth's Minority Partner
In its Blue Marble project, the U.S. space agency NASA is combining photographs of the planet taken by its Terra and Aqua satellites to create a montage portrait of Earth. Most of the photos used were shot during clear weather in order to present a remarkably clear view of the planet. But the portrait is also not representative, since it does not show the extent to which clouds swathe portions of the planet on a typical day. The Blue Marble portrait at left, centered on the eastern Pacific Ocean, shows the extent to which Earth's surface is covered by oceans rather than land.

Making Waves

MARINERS HAVE BEEN CHARTING THE TIDES, THE REGULAR RISE AND FALL IN THE ELEVATION of the oceans' surface, since humans first went down to the sea in ships. But it wasn't until the 17th century that pioneering physicist Isaac Newton began to illuminate the forces that drive the tides. Newton's laws of gravitation explained the daily rise and fall of the seas as a result of the mutually attractive force exerted by the moon and Earth upon each other. As is sometimes overlooked, the sun's gravity also plays a role in the flow of the tides. The moon's gravitational tug deforms both the fluid seas and the solid part of the planet, causing the side of Earth nearest the satellite to bulge out toward it. At the same time, the centrifugal force created by the planet's rotation causes a second bulge on the side farthest from the moon, causing both the oceans and the planet's crust to rise slightly as they vainly attempt to slingshot into space. As the planet spins, both land and sea rotate through these bulges, making ocean levels rise and fall, in most cases resulting in two high tides and two low tides each day.

Gravity, one of nature's unseen yet powerful wonders, has other tricks to play with the tides. The sun is far larger than Earth and the moon, but because it is so distant from us, it exerts only 46% of the gravitational pull of the moon. Yet when the two bodies align in relation to Earth, at the time of the full and new moons, they exert a much increased force on the oceans, creating larger high tides and smaller low tides. Just to add a dash of confusion, these regular increases are called spring tides, though they aren't related to the season of spring.

But wait—there's more! As the moon revolves around Earth about every 29 days, it moves the tidal clock about 50 minutes later each day. And did we mention that the size of a tide in a given location is also affected by the shape of the coastline, the depth of the water and the shape of the seafloor in a given location? That's a lot of physics to absorb, but when these theoretical concepts are seen in visible form, the results can be remarkable—as they are each day at Nova Scotia's Bay of Fundy. Due to the long narrow shape of the bay's natural harbor, which magnifies the tidal force, the level of the ocean along the coast of the bay can vary by as much as 56 ft. between tides. So when "surf's up!" … it's *way* up, dudes! ■

The surge *A full moon sets over the rocky shore of Laguna Beach, Calif. The interaction of celestial bodies causes the regular ebb and flow of the oceans' tides, but the physical formation of a given locale also plays a part in determining the extent of the tidal range*

Talking Tides: A Glossary

Ebb Tide: Receding water as low tide sets in

Full Moon: Phase of moon when it is on the opposite side of the Earth from the sun and full surface is visible

Neap Tide: The monthly period of smallest tidal range, caused by the opposition of the moon and the sun

New Moon: Phase of moon when it lies between Earth and sun with dark side facing our planet, and thus is not visible

Semidiurnal Tide: By far the most common tidal cycle: two high and two low tides each day

Slack Water/Slack Tide: When high tide ceases and low tide begins; also called the turning of the tide

Spring Tide: The monthly period of highest and lowest tides, caused by the alignment of the moon and the sun

Syzygy: The alignment of Earth, the moon and the sun in a straight line that creates spring tide conditions

Tidal Range: The measurement of the size of the tides; the difference between the height of the ocean level at high and low tides

Beachwear: Basic Black

LIKE YELLOWSTONE NATIONAL PARK, ICELAND offers us a chance to view a freshly created world, where the enormous forces that drive the planet but are often hidden from view—clashing tectonic plates, belching volcanoes and sizzling hydrothermal activity—are operating at full tilt, unusually close to the earth's skin. The beautifully eerie black sand beach on the Dyrhólaey Peninsula, above, is a clear signal that this is no ordinary landscape: the shore here is composed of the remnants of hot, flowing lava that cooled and shattered into particles when it entered the sea. (Geologists also recognize an entirely different form of black sand, a mineral-rich, heavy particulate that is deposited by glacial activity.) Far across the world, Punaluu Beach on the island of Hawaii has a similar ebony coastline, as do shorelines formed by volcanoes on other islands around the planet.

Like Iceland, the world's coastlines are among the most dynamic areas on the planet. This border zone between the hydrosphere and the pedosphere is constantly in change, swept and shaped by tides and winds. Coastlines can be formed in various ways: some are volcanic in origin, like Dyrhólaey. Others are river deltas, muddy alluvial plains formed by sediments carried downstream and deposited at the ocean's doorway. Coasts formed by land activity are primary coasts; secondary coasts are those created by the action of the sea. The south coast of England and east coast of Australia are secondary coasts where rising sea levels have flooded former valleys; scientists refer to such areas as drowned or submerged coasts. As the melting of glaciers in polar zones accelerates, scientists fear that drowned coasts may no longer be mere marvels but a threat to millions living near ocean shorelines. ■

Data Stream: Iceland lies directly on top of the Mid-Atlantic Ridge, where two tectonic plates collide • The

Washed Away

Coastal erosion is a battle between land and sea in which the dynamic sea is always the winner in the end. At left, great shards of rock have fallen from coastal cliffs in Hunstanton, England, victims of the constant battering of the surf and wind—exposing a fine horizontal study in sedimentary rock patterns. Although ocean waves usually wear away coasts, in some places they can actually create new land by depositing sediment over time (as many rivers do), in a process called coastal deposition.

peninsula of Dyrhólaey was originally a distinct island but it later merged with the main body of Iceland

Hidden Realms

I T'S THE STUFF OF SCIENCE FICTION, *SEINFELD* OR STRING THEORY: imagine a world that is hidden from our view yet runs parallel to our own, if composed in a slightly different key. There is such a world, of course, and it's surprising how little we know about it: the world of the ocean depths and the seabeds of the planet's oceans. The wonders of this hidden realm are manifold. They include a gash that cuts more than six miles (9.5 km) deep into the earth's crust. They include tectonic rifts far longer and more active than those found on land. They include 90% of the the planet's active volcanoes. They include its highest mountain: only the top 13,796 ft. (4,205 m) of Hawaii's Mauna Kea stand above sea level, but its total height from sea floor to summit is 33,465 feet (10,200 meters), dwarfing Mount Everest. And they include bizarre life-forms: the mysterious giant squid; luminescent fish adapted to life under enormous pressure; big tube worms that cluster around steaming hydrothermal vents miles beneath the waves.

The seabeds of the oceans are the planet's most active tectonic region. The largest single geological feature on the earth is the 40,000-mile (65,000 km) -long mountain chain known as the Mid-Oceanic Ridge, which winds around the planet along the borders where tectonic plates meet. The ridge, which varies in height, is constantly being replenished by hot magma that flows to the surface as lava, then hardens to form oceanic crust. At other points where plates meet, one plate is subducted beneath the other, creating a deep-sea trench. The deepest place in the ocean lies in the Mariana Trench in the Pacific Ocean; the 35,800-ft. (10,900 m) abyss was named the Challenger Trench, for the submersible craft that first probed it. Prescription: more probing of these hidden realms is long overdue. ■

Hot Springs Under the Sea

In 1979 a group of scientists aboard the submersible craft Alvin *became the first to see a phenomenon discovered by instruments two years before: hydrothermal vents on the ocean floor off the Galápagos Islands at a depth of 1.8 miles (2.9 km). The vents operate much like hot springs on the surface, allowing heated, mineral-rich water from beneath the crust to flow into the ocean. Some of these vents, like the one at left, form chimneys made of hardened minerals. The scientists also found tube worms and spider crabs living near the vents.*

Subaqueous galaxy *A diver in an ice cave beneath the Weddell Sea, part of the Southern Ocean in Antarctica, illuminates a group of colorful starfish lying on the seabed*

43

Undersea Treasure?

COULD THE SOLUTION TO THE WORLD'S ENERGY problems lie within the ocean's seabeds? U.S. Geological Survey (USGS) researcher Tim Collett believes that may be the case. "This is potentially a revolutionary energy resource," he told TIME in 2008, referring to natural gas hydrates, the icelike formations of methane suspended within a cage of solidified water molecules that are found in deep oceans and beneath permafrost around the world. Long theorized to exist in the outer solar system, methane hydrates were discovered on Earth in the 1930s, when they began forming spontaneously inside natural-gas pipelines that ran through cold regions. In the 1960s they were first found in nature, thanks to new forms of radar that could penetrate the ground and the sea floor.

"Hydrates are formed from the interaction of gas and water," Collett explains. "When methane vents from the earth's interior and hits a layer of water at low temperature and high pressure, they become locked together." The result is a crystalline structure that looks like dirty snow and feels like slushy ice. But this is no ordinary frost. "If you hold a piece of gas hydrate up to your ear," he says, "you can actually hear it hissing and spitting as the methane escapes. And if you expose it to a flame, it will flare intensely until all the gas is burned off." Part of what gives gas hydrates their punch is what geologists call their "energy density"—a cubic centimeter of methane hydrate contains 164 times as much energy as the same volume of ordinary natural gas.

So how much energy does all this fiery ice hold? "Conservative estimates say the total energy contained in all the world's hydrates is more than all known oil, coal and natural gas on the planet combined," says Collett. "And some scientists believe that the total might be two or three times higher than that." Indeed, a single field of hydrates off the coast of North Carolina is believed to contain enough methane to meet all U.S. energy demands for more than a century.

So why aren't we all driving cars powered by exploding snowballs? Because most hydrates are found where they're hard to get: buried deep in permafrost and even deeper under seabeds, below 1,000 ft. (305 m) of water. This makes the costs of extraction high. There are also serious environmental concerns to address. Methane is a potent greenhouse gas, trapping solar heat 10 to 20 times as effectively as carbon dioxide. If accidentally vented into the atmosphere during hydrate recovery, methane could speed the effects of global warming. Another risk: continental shelves honeycombed with hydrates could become destabilized by extraction, perhaps triggering underwater landslides and tsunamis. Yet there's also an ecological upside. "Natural gas burns much more cleanly than other fossil fuels. If handled properly, methane hydrates could help us cut pollution significantly," explains Collett.

"Nobody knows for sure yet what proportion of a hydrate deposit can be extracted economically," Collett concludes, acknowledging that some of it may not be recoverable at any price. "But the amounts are so huge that if even a small percentage of it can be made practical to use, this could be world-changing stuff." ∎

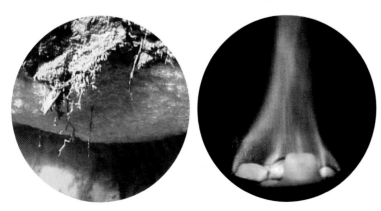

Fire, Ice and Energy

Tim Collett led a USGS team on a 2008 expedition to India, which discovered in the Krishna-Godavari Basin one of the richest marine gas hydrate fields yet identified. The team also established a new prototype hydrate-extraction facility in the Bay of Bengal. At far left is a slab of gas hydrate photographed beneath the waves; at near left, solidified pieces of methane extracted from gas hydrates burn off.

Collett estimates that profitable extraction of gas hydrates and distribution of the methane they contain are some 10 to 15 years away, with nations short on energy resources, like India and Japan, leading the process.

45

Kingdoms of Coral

THE GREAT BARRIER REEF THAT LIES OFF THE EAST coast of Australia is one of the largest natural wonders of the planet. Then again, coral reefs by definition are wonders in themselves, for unlike waterfalls or hot springs or rock pinnacles, they are formed not by inorganic natural processes but by living creatures: they are the remains of small marine organisms. The coral polyps whose hard exoskeletons combine to form a reef are tiny indeed: an individual polyp is only about 0.03 in. (1 to 3 mm) long. The Great Barrier Reef, on the other hand, is massive: it stretches for 2,300 miles (1,430 km) along the east coast of Queensland.

The dichotomy between the minute polyps and the vast structure they form is accounted for by the other essential factor in the shaping of reefs: eons of time. The Great Barrier Reef we see today began to take shape some 9,000 years ago, forming exoskeleton by exoskeleton on the remains of an earlier reef that scientists believe was in place as long as 600,000 year ago.

Coral polyps, also known as hard or stony corals, generally live in communities. They feed on tiny plankton in the ocean and also absorb nutrition from algae that dwell in their tissues, secreting calcium carbonate as they grow. Because they flourish in very

TOP: YANN ARTHUS-BERTRAND—CORBIS; RIGHT: NORBERT

Bright Orange—For Now
The Great Barrier Reef is alive not only with the beautifully tinted corals that have built it but also with fantastically colored fish like the coral trout at left, a type of grouper that can change its colors to foil predators. Habitats for a wide variety of fish and shellfish, coral reefs are the keystones of oceanic ecosystems that are a primary food source for tens of millions of people who live along the world's coastlines. Above, a few of the shallow coral reefs that make up Australia's enormous natural wonder.

specific conditions—requiring sunlight, clear water warmed to 64° to 88°F (18° to 31°C) and a minimum of severe wave action—corals are confined to tropical and subtropical areas of the globe.

Reefs assume a wide variety of forms. Fringe reefs are those that form a ring attached to the shore of a tropical island, sometimes with a lagoon between the reef and shore. Barrier reefs grow parallel to the shores of continents, with a deep lagoon between reef and shore. Australia's mighty reef forms a beautiful necklace around the northeast coast of the continent, a coral archipelago made up of almost 3,000 distinct reefs and

some 900 islands in the Coral Sea. But like smaller reefs all across the planet, the Great Barrier Reef is threatened by climate change: warmer ocean waters lead to a process called coral bleaching in which the algae coral use for nutrition die off, leaving behind colorless, dead corals. Major bleaching events struck this reef in 1998, 2002 and 2006; more can be expected. Scientists say the coral reefs to Australia's west in the Indian Ocean are even more seriously endangered owing to warming seas; indeed, the ongoing rapid decline of coral reefs around the planet is one of the most unsettling signs of global climate change. ■

Rings in the Ocean

Atoll, Palau, South Pacific

Atolls are oceanic treasures, hiding in plain sight. The term *atolls* was coined by South Pacific islanders for these unique circular or elliptically shaped reefs that grace the island archipelagoes in their region. For scientists, atolls posed a mystery that required more than 100 years to solve. The problem: they are composed of coral reefs whose older sections extend well under the surface, whereas corals, by their nature, can only live in shallow waters, where the tiny creatures that build them can receive the sunlight they need to live. The Sherlock Holmes of the atoll was naturalist Charles Darwin. During his voyage aboard the H.M.S. *Beagle* in the 1830s, he studied atolls and reached a surprising conclusion: they are built on the remnants of extinct volcanoes, and the corals are latecomers in the process that forms them.

Darwin noticed that atolls seem to exist in three stages of development. In its first stage, an atoll is a fringe reef forming around the slopes of a volcano. Next, an atoll forms a barrier reef that encircles the volcano, much of whose substance is submerged below the waves, deeper than coral reefs can live. In its third stage the volcano is entirely submerged, and a ring of coral reef forms around a central lagoon. Darwin argued that atolls form as volcanoes slowly subside into the ocean. The hypothesis fit the stages—except for its argument that volcanoes could somehow sink beneath the waves. It wasn't until the theory of plate tectonics was accepted, more than 100 years after Darwin's voyage, that scientists realized that extinct volcanoes could indeed subside into the sea, as they cool and contract, or as the giant tectonic plates that compose the planet's crust slowly move and shift locations. Elementary! ∎

Data Stream: The Pacific Ocean is home to most of the world's atolls, owing to the volcanic Ring of Fire that

Great Blue Hole, Lighthouse Reef, Belize

An atoll is a coral reef forming a circle or ellipse that surrounds the remnants of a submerged, extinct volcano. But not all the graceful rings in the ocean are atolls. Consider one of the loveliest sights in the Caribbean Sea, the Great Blue Hole off Lighthouse Reef, east of Belize. This deep-blue circle, almost entirely surrounded by a reef, seems to offer a portal to the oceanic underworld. Indeed, it is has been measured to be 410 ft. (125 m) deep, even though the waters in its vicinity are very shallow, like many of the coastal shelves off the isles of the Caribbean.

What's going on? The Great Blue Hole is an example of a phenomenon that occurs in both the hydrosphere and the pedosphere: it is a sinkhole. Like sinkholes on land—the kind common in regions of karst topography that seem to appear without warning, bent on swallowing homes—it was initially formed as a void in a limestone cave system. During the last Ice Age, which ended about 10,000 years ago, the Great Blue Hole and the area around it were above land. But when melting ice filled the planet's oceans with water, the cave system was submerged. Sometime later, in a process that echoed those that formed the cavelike cenotes not far away in Mexico, the roof of the cavern collapsed, and the vast space filled with water: the Great Blue Hole.

Some 1,000 ft. (305 m) wide, this ring of bright water has become one of the most sought-after sites in the world for scuba divers; indeed, the inventor of the scuba apparatus that made undersea exploration a popular sport, Jacques-Yves Cousteau, was one of the first to probe its splendors. ■

Lifeline

AGRICULTURE AND SOCIETY ASSUME A LINEAR form in Egypt, as towns and farms cluster along the edges of northern Africa's life-bringing river, the Nile. The band of fertility, replenished annually by the river's famed floods, extends to an average of only about 1 mile (1.5 km) on either side of the river. This blue ribbon cutting through brown desert terrain is less than 5% of Egypt's total land area, but more than 95% of Egyptians live along the Nile floodplain.

The Nile is the longest river in the world, at 4,132 miles (6,650 km), and it drains an enormous swath of northern Africa, thanks to its two powerful tributaries, the White Nile and the Blue Nile. The White Nile, the longer of the two, flows from high in the mountains of Rwanda across Tanzania, through Lake Victoria and down through Uganda and Sudan, where its flow is severely retarded as it passes through the marshlands of the Sudd. The Blue Nile lies to the east of the White Nile, flowing from the highlands around Lake Tana in Ethiopia down into Sudan, where it joins the White Nile at Khartoum, one of the planet's great river-junction cities. It is by far the larger contributor, making up some 84% of the Nile's total flow.

Rivers play a key role in irrigating the planet, and since humans need freshwater to survive, ancient societies often first took root along their shores. As the world's population has boomed, the need for ever increasing supplies of water has turned control of river waters into a major political and economic battle-ground. When a dispute over water rights between the states of Georgia, Alabama and Florida could not be settled by federal officials in 2008, it was referred to the U.S. Supreme Court. The usage of the water in the Colorado River has spawned recurring problems between the U.S. and Mexico. And in March 2008, 10 northern African nations began meeting in Uganda in hopes of settling ongoing disputes about the use of the water flowing in the Nile and its tributaries.

Small wonder: the annual floods along the Nile, like the monsoons of South Asia, are one of the planet's great ongoing processes of hydrologic renewal, channeling not only freshwater but also rich, soil-building silt into an otherwise arid landscape. The broad, lush, fan-shaped delta where the Nile flows into the Mediterranean Sea is composed of soil borne from mountains thousands of miles away. Freshwater and silt are the twin pillars upon which early Egyptians created one of mankind's first great civilizations, while another of the river's gifts, the sedge plant papyrus, provided the Pharaohs' chroniclers with the medium to brag about their deeds. ■

Dusk and dunes *The building of the Aswan High Dam in the 1960s created Lake Nasser, a huge reservoir that extends into both Egypt and Sudan*

Life Along the Nile

The historic civilization of Egypt was made possible by the Nile, and thousands of years later the river is just as essential to life in northern Africa. The photo above of fellucas gracing the river at Aswan illustrates the ruthless dichotomy that prevails along its banks, as arid desert sand dunes tower over the river, which may be thought of as a sort of long, narrow oasis.

When Egypt erected the controversial Aswan High Dam in the 1960s, it was the first time human intervention had significantly altered the flow of the Nile, moderating the extent of its annual floods in hopes of stabilizing irrigation and preventing disasters. At left, a boy waters his horse in the river. At right is a Nubian village upriver, in Sudan, where the Nile's two tributaries unite.

Artery of a Continent

LIKE MANY OF THE PLANET'S GREAT RIVERS, THE Amazon is the offspring of a mammoth mountain range. But the Amazon doesn't merely drain the great snows of the Andes; its history has been shaped by them. The mountains, formed by the clash of two tectonic plates, thrust a rocky barrier, or cordillera, as high as 20,000 ft. (6,096 m) along the entire west side of the South American continent. As a result, rains that fell on the eastern slopes of these mountains, though less than 100 miles (160 km) from the Pacific Ocean in some cases, needed to drain across the entire width of the continent to reach the Atlantic. Initially they flowed into a giant inland sea in the center of South America, but at some point within the past 2 million years, these waters rose high enough to break free to the east, and the Amazon was born. The sedimentary basin of the former sea became one of the earth's great tropical rain forests, and again the Andes played a part, trapping moist winds from the jungle and sending them back as rain clouds in a fertile feedback loop.

This massive waterway is by far the largest river on the planet, though the Nile is a tad longer. It drains an astounding 40% of South America's landmass and plays a major role in ventilating the entire globe. In a 2005 study published in *Nature* magazine, researchers found that the Amazon and its tributaries are "breathing" more quickly than was previously thought. The vegetation of the Amazon basin absorbs carbon dioxide, retains it, converts it into oxygen and releases it in a cycle lasting an average of only five years. Earlier, scientists had believed this cycle took decades, even centuries. If the Amazon and the rain forests it feeds are the heart of the planet's cardiopulmonary system, then our planet's pulse seems to be racing. ∎

Great Rivers of the World

The Nile is longer than the Amazon, but the latter carries more water to the sea than any other river on Earth. Here are the next four largest rivers on the planet, measured by the amount of water they discharge at their mouths.

Congo The largest river in central Africa feeds a great rain forest, draining from the East African rift into the Atlantic. Its watershed is a bit larger than that of the Mississippi, the largest of North American rivers.

Yangtze The longest river in Asia is the traditional line that divides north and south China. Its watershed stretches from a glacier high in the Tibetan plateau to Shanghai, where it flows into the East China Sea.

Orinoco South America's other great river lies in the north, carrying water from Colombia and Venezuela into the Atlantic just south of the Caribbean Sea.

Brahmaputra The headwaters of South Asia's great river are in the glacier fields of the Himalayas. The river meets India's mighty Ganges to form a vast delta in Bangladesh.

Come Together

Two great rivers converge near Manaus, the largest city on the Amazon, some 800 miles (1,290 km) upriver from the Atlantic. The muddy river on the left is the Amazon, its waters laden with silt; the blue-black stream is the Rio Negro, largest of the Amazon's tributaries. The Rio Negro is a blackwater river: it has a deep, slow-moving channel, runs through swamps and wetlands and is darkened by decaying vegetable matter. At right, the Amazon snakes through the rain forest in western Brazil.

CLAUS MEYER—MINDEN PICTURES

Perched water table
A freshwater spring cascades down a hillside in Olympia National Park in Washington State, surrounded by mosses, ferns and other plants that flourish where fresh running water is abundant

Gushers

A GREEN GLEN DEEP IN THE FOREST, WITH FRESH, clear water bursting from an unseen source and cascading down a hillside: Is there a more apt symbol for the mysterious yet essential forces of nature that sustain the miracle of life on our planet? Freshwater springs offer us an opportunity to glimpse, feel and taste a primary aspect of the earth's hydrologic cycle: groundwater. Water is everywhere on the globe, in a dazzling variety of forms and locations. Oceans, rivers and lakes hold a good deal of the planet's water. The frozen world of the cryosphere holds even more water in the form of ice. Above our heads, clouds are concentrations of condensed water vapor, and there's also a good deal of water vapor that we don't see in the atmosphere, operating as part of the process of transpiration, which keeps the planet breathing.

Yet there's another repository of water that's so close to us it's easy to overlook: the ground beneath our feet holds an estimated 30% of all the freshwater on the globe, far more than is held in its rivers, lakes and atmosphere combined. Under the surface of the planet, water lies in two distinct zones: the top layer is called the zone of aeration, where the soil is not completely saturated by water. This is the area where plants and trees root and farmers cultivate the soil. The bottom layer is called the zone of saturation; the water that makes up most of its mass is called groundwater. The upper part of this zone of saturation is called the water table; it is into this area that humans dig wells to find water under sufficient pressure to be brought to the surface. In some cases, though, the usually unseen water table intersects with the surface of the planet, and groundwater gushes forth, seemingly from no distinct source: a surprise, a delight, a spring. ∎

Water Words: A Glossary

Aquifer An underground layer of permeable matter, such as sand or gravel, in which water moves freely.

Aquitard An underground layer of impermeable matter, such as clay, that hinders water movement.

Geyser A spring that intermittently releases water from below the ground that is heated and under pressure with an eruptive force.

Hot spring A spring that releases groundwater heated by underground geothermal activity.

Perched water table A localized zone of saturation within a zone of aeration that acts as an aquifer and collects water. Water tables perched in the ground in hillsides explain the flow of water from high above the surface, as seen in the photo at left.

Cataraction

POLAR AURORAS AND THE OCEANS' TIDES ARE NATURAL phenomena created by forces that are vast, unseen and mind-boggling. But there's not much mystery involved in the operation of a waterfall. The recipe is simple: take a stream of running water; add a sudden, sharp drop in ground level. But when the running stream is the Zambezi River in southern Africa and the sudden descent involves a vertical drop of 360 ft. (109 m), running along a horizontal face about 1 mile (1.6 km) long—the result is Victoria Falls, one of the great wonders of the planet. Sorry, Niagara: this cataract along the border of Zambia and Zimbabwe is both much higher and much wider than the famed waterfall shared by Canada and the U.S. But because Victoria Falls reflects the seasonal flow of the Zambezi, shrinking to a series of separate falls in the summer dry season, much more water flows over Niagara Falls each year. The planet's third-largest cataract, Iguazu Falls in Argentina and Brazil, is one-third again as wide as Victoria but not nearly as tall.

British missionary and explorer David Livingstone was the first European to behold Victoria Falls, in 1855; he christened them for his Queen. Africans call the falls Mosi-oa-Tunya: "the Smoke That Thunders." And thunder it does in the rainy season, when some 38,000 cu. ft. of water takes the plunge each second. On nights when the full moon is bright, another of nature's wonders can be seen in the mist of the falls: a shimmering moonbow. ∎

Waterfall Words: A Glossary

Cascade A waterfall that traverses several distinct steps in its descent

Cataract Any large waterfall or one with whose current flows swiftly

Horsetail A trickling fall whose water maintains contact with the underlying bedrock in its descent

Plunge A fall whose water loses contact with the bedrock surface in its descent, as in both Victoria and Niagara falls

Plunge Pool A deep trough that forms where the descending water hits the lower stream

Rock Shelter A cavelike opening behind the lower section of a plunge waterfall that forms when softer rock below a harder upper layer is eroded by the flow of the water

abundant spray from the waterfall creates a rain-forest microclimate in its immediate vicinity

A Crater Made Greater

SUPERLATIVES SEEM SUPERFLUOUS WHEN DEALING with a geological wonder on the scale of Crater Lake. This unique relic of a volcanic eruption is breathtaking for its scenic setting alone: high in the Cascade Mountain range in Oregon, some 6,178 ft. (1,883 m) above sea level, it is surrounded by cliffs and cradled in a mountaintop. As visitors gaze six miles across the lake's deep-blue water to the other side, they see the peaked hat of Wizard Island in the middle of the pool. This island is actually the cinder cone left behind in the eruption that formed the caldera.

The lake was formed an estimated 7,000 years ago following the eruption of Mount Mazama, which scientists believe was one of the largest such blasts in the history of North America. The big bang blew off the top of the mountain, thought to have then been 12,000 ft. (3,657 m) high, spreading magma, ash and debris across tens of thousands of square miles. After the eruption, what was left of the mountain collapsed into the huge void of its former magma chamber. Mazama was now half its former size, and the caldera on its summit filled up with water: Crater Lake.

Conehead *Wizard Island, at left, is the top of a volcanic cone that formed after Mount Mazama erupted; a smaller cone lies beneath the lake's surface*

Legendary Lakes

Here are a few of the planet's more fascinating lakes, based on size, depth, location and other factors:

Great Lakes The largest system of freshwater lakes in the world is composed of five big lakes that constitute a vast inland sea along the U.S.-Canada border. They were formed by glacial action following the Ice Age 10,000 years ago.

Lake Baikal The deepest lake in the world, at 5,716 ft. (1,741 m), this Siberian lake is also one of the world's oldest; it formed along a tectonic fault line some 25 million years ago.

Lake Titicaca The largest freshwater lake in South America is the highest major lake in the world: it lies 12,507 ft. (3,182 m) above sea level in the Andes, bordering Bolivia and Peru.

Some of the lake's most fascinating aspects lie below its surface. Because its waters are extremely clear, sunlight penetrates deep within it: fields of moss spread along the shallower slopes on its sides and can be found even at depths of 460 ft. (140 m). Much farther down, on its bottom—at 1,943 ft. (592 m), Crater is the deepest lake in the U.S.—it boasts another oddity: bacteria colonies grow around hydrothermal vents that release hot water into the depths. This process, which duplicates conditions at the bottom of the planet's oceans, is taking place inside a mountain.

What separates a pond from a lake? In this case, size matters, and the dividing line is not scientifically precise: a lake is simply a large pond. Most of the world's lakes are freshwater, though a few, like the Dead Sea and the Great Salt Lake, are saline. Many lakes are very young in geological terms, for they formed in basins carved by glaciers retreating after the most recent Ice Age, 10,000 years ago. Other lakes, like Scotland's Loch Ness, formed when waters filled chasms along tectonic divides. And a few others, like Crater, fill volcanic caldera: crown jewels among the world's big ponds. ■

Old Salts

FEELING DOWN? KEEP YOUR DISTANCE FROM THE Dead Sea in the Middle East, whose shoreline makes up the single lowest region on the surface of the land planet. (Mariana Trench in the Pacific is the lowest point beneath the oceans.) It's 1,378 ft. (420 m) below sea level here, and that sinking feeling visitors experience is for real: the level of the water in this salt lake has been shrinking slowly since the body of water first assumed its present shape some 10,000 years ago, and its size is declining as well. In its desert setting between Israel and Jordan, solar heat evaporates its water faster than the 4 in. (10 cm) of annual rainfall and inflow from the Jordan River can replenish it.

As for that water, the Dead Sea is one of the world's largest saline lakes. (The names of seas and lakes can be deceiving; a sea is properly a distinct portion of a saltwater ocean, but the Dead Sea was named long before modern geographers arrived at definitions.) Salt makes up about one-third of its waters, giving its surface the buoyant quality that tourists find so uplifting. By comparison, the world's oceans are a 3% saline solution, while the salinity of Utah's Great Salt Lake is variable, ranging from 5% to 27%. The salt deposits here are ancient indeed; an early form of the Dead Sea, which geologists call Lake Sodom, was formed upon salt deposits more than 1 mile (0.6 km) deep.

Like Loch Ness in Scotland, the Dead Sea took shape when sea waters filled a rift valley, in this case the boundary at which the Arabian and African tectonic plates moved away from each other. The outlet to the sea later closed, making the Dead Sea one of the world's endorheic, or terminal, lakes: one that has no outlet. Technically, it is part of the same Great Rift Valley that snakes across eastern Africa and up through the Middle East to Syria. At times in its past, it has been both far larger and far higher than it is today; about 26,000 years ago, it suffered a dramatic drop in elevation, most likely owing to some sort of major seismic event, scientists believe.

Recently the Dead Sea has been shrinking at a rapid pace, as water flow from the Jordan River has been reduced by irrigation and lack of rainfall. The Lisan Peninsula, which divides the sea into northern and southern sections, may soon become the southern shoreline of the lake, and its southern arm may become a salt flat. And as for flora and fauna: it's called the Dead Sea because its salinity makes it unfit for almost all plants and animals, though a few types of bacteria, fungi and algae cling to life in its forbidding waters. But if you're looking for asphalt, you've come to the right place: small pebbles of the black stuff now and then are vented from the planet's crust at the bottom of this remarkable body of water. ∎

Unique Lakes

Great Salt Lake, Utah
Salt Lake City's eponym is the largest saline lake in the western hemisphere. It is all that remains of a far larger body of water, Lake Bonneville, which at one time covered most of the surface of the Great Basin region of the West. Today, like parts of the Dead Sea, the former lakebed has become a vast, dry desert region, the Bonneville Salt Flats, where the surface salt deposits are as much as 6 ft. (1.8 m) deep in places.

Lake Nyos, Cameroon
Like Oregon's Crater Lake, this body of water was formed in the crater of an extinct volcano. In 1986 large quantities of carbon dioxide were released from the bottom of the lake by a still unknown seismic event, killing some 1,800 people. Since 1990 scientists have been working to de-gas the lake.

Dead but still dying *Due to the reduced size of the Dead Sea in recent years, its southern portion is in peril of becoming a vast salt flat*

Still Holding Up

The buoyancy of the Dead Sea is one of nature's paradoxes: we expect water to feel porous and, well, liquid, rather than as viscous as a pudding. But sure enough, the lakewater serves as its own flotation device, to the delight of tourists, right. Of more interest to scientists: the viscosity of the water also retards circulation, making the waters of the lake highly stratified. Since there is little vertical circulation in the lake, the Dead Sea is a sort of time capsule, much like bedrock on land: the water near the bottom of the 1,084-ft. (330 m) lake is far older than the water at its top.

As with many hot springs and salt lakes, the waters of the Dead Sea are regarded as therapeutic by many people because of their high mineral content.

Slow-Motion Flood

LOCALS CALL THE EVERGLADES, FLORIDA'S GREAT subtropical wetlands, the "river of grass," a term made popular by pioneering environmentalist Marjory Stoneman Douglas. The description is accurate, but visitors to this fascinating ecosystem find nothing resembling a river; it is just as accurate to describe the Everglades as a slow-moving flood. This vast marsh, now encompassing some 18,000 sq. mi. (46,619 sq km) of land, drains most of the Florida peninsula, from the Kissimmee River in the north down through Lake Okeechobee to Florida Bay. The Everglades proper extends from Okeechobee to the Gulf; the marshy area was once twice its current size, but although the rising tide of human development in the region has downsized this natural wonder, it remains a unique feature of the North American continent.

This shallow river moves across the limestone bedrock surface at the stately pace of about a quarter-mile (0.4 km) a day, in a process scientists call sheet-flow. The predominant plant here is sawgrass, a sedge whose sharp blades make travel difficult for humans but serve as dandy alligator nests. Wildlife is increas-ingly imperiled but hanging on; Everglades National Park is home to 24 species that are endangered or threatened, including the Florida panther, the West Indian manatee and the American crocodile. Its chang-ing ecology attracts newcomers. Burmese pythons, which can grow to 20 ft. in length, are spreading rapid-ly; the number captured in the park reached nearly 250 in 2007, and the population is growing.

As TIME reported in 2007, the Everglades has been an endangered site ever since the U.S. Army Corps of Engineers started draining and diverting it in the mid-20th century, trashing eons of delicate natural plumb-ing to make way for sugar farms and ranch houses. One result: an astonishing 90% of the Everglades' wading bird population has disappeared. Only in 2000 did the Florida and Federal governments finally seem to acknowledge that the Everglades was not a swamp but a unique and vital ecosystem. They embarked on a $10 billion, 20-year project to restore the Everglades to something like its original state. But the plan remains under constant challenge, driven by Florida's long struggle between development and conservation. ■

An arbor in the glade *Cypress tree marshes are only one of the many distinct ecosystems that coexist within the Everglades, which is also home to mangrove swamps, salt marshes and estuaries*

Creatures of the Everglades

The American alligator (Alligator mississippiensis), *above, is one of only two gator species on the planet; the Chinese alligator is now reduced to very small numbers along the Yangtze River and is considered highly endangered. At right is a tricolored heron, also known as the Louisiana heron, which lives in colonies on platform nests built of sticks. Herons are among the wading shorebirds that are threatened by loss of native habitat in the Everglades.*

to some 80 to 100 endangered Florida panthers • Fires sparked by lightning keep its plant life in balance

Amphibious World

MANGROVE SWAMPS ARE AMONG THE PLANET'S most unique, self-contained and fascinating ecosystems. Here is a world of humid, hushed spaces, where dappled sunlight dances on the water, the silence is interrupted by the sound of scuttling crabs, and the scenery consists of swampy water, ropy vines and twisted roots—except where the vines are twisted and the roots are ropy. The term *mangrove* is used somewhat indiscriminately: it can refer to all the varieties of trees and shrubs of the habitat that scientists call a mangal, but it is also commonly used to refer to the mangrove tree, genus *Rhizophora.*

Like the mangal itself, these trees have a dual nature: they are adapted to life on the margin of the sea and the land. Their multiple stilt (or prop) roots elevate the trees' foliage above the water, allowing the leaves to breathe; in some cases the roots are able to filter out salt in the seawater they take in, while in others the leaves are able to excrete excess salt. Like rainforests, to which they are often compared, these swamps play an important role in the planet's carbon cycle, taking in carbon from the atmosphere. Mangals play a key role in reducing coastal erosion; they also protect coasts from tsunamis by reducing the impact of storm surges. Yet scientists estimate that increased human encroachment has reduced the size of these important buffer zones along tropical coast-lines as much as 20% in recent decades. ■

Nosing around *At left, three lemon shark pups prowl among the stilt roots of mangrove trees in a mangal in the Bimini Islands*

Denizens of the Mangal

Mangrove swamps are home to a number of highly adapted species, some of which cannot survive outside the saltwater mangal habitat.

Crustaceans
Crabs, shrimp, barnacles, oysters, mussels, prawns
Note: In recent years, one direct threat to mangrove habitats has been human aquaculture, due to the explosive growth of artificial shrimp ponds in mangrove areas

Fish
Sea bass, tilapia, mudskipper, archerfish, grouper, shark

Trees
Red, white, black and sweet mangroves; perepat

Plants
Ferns, mosses, mangrove liverwort
Note: Plants that are adapted to living in saltwater environments are called halophytes

Birds
Pelican, heron, egret, plover, sandpiper, kingfisher, woodpecker

Animals
Alligator, crocodile, water snakes, geckos, pit viper, frog

Open Wide!
Like mangrove trees, mangrove crabs are well adapted to their half-land, half-sea environment. At left is one of the larger such crabs, Scylla serrata, *whose shell width in males is usually around 8.5 in. (22 cm) in size. Also known as a mud crab or black crab, this jumbo-sized crustacean lives in Africa, Asia and Australia, where it is a major food source for millions of people. The crabs also play a key role in breaking down decayed vegetable matter in the swamps, which helps feed the algae, bacteria and other minute creatures that make up the mangrove habitat.*

65

pedosphere

pe·do·sphere *(n.)*
[Gk *pedon* ground, earth + Gk *sphaira* ball]
the part of the earth's surface that contains the soil layer;
the land world

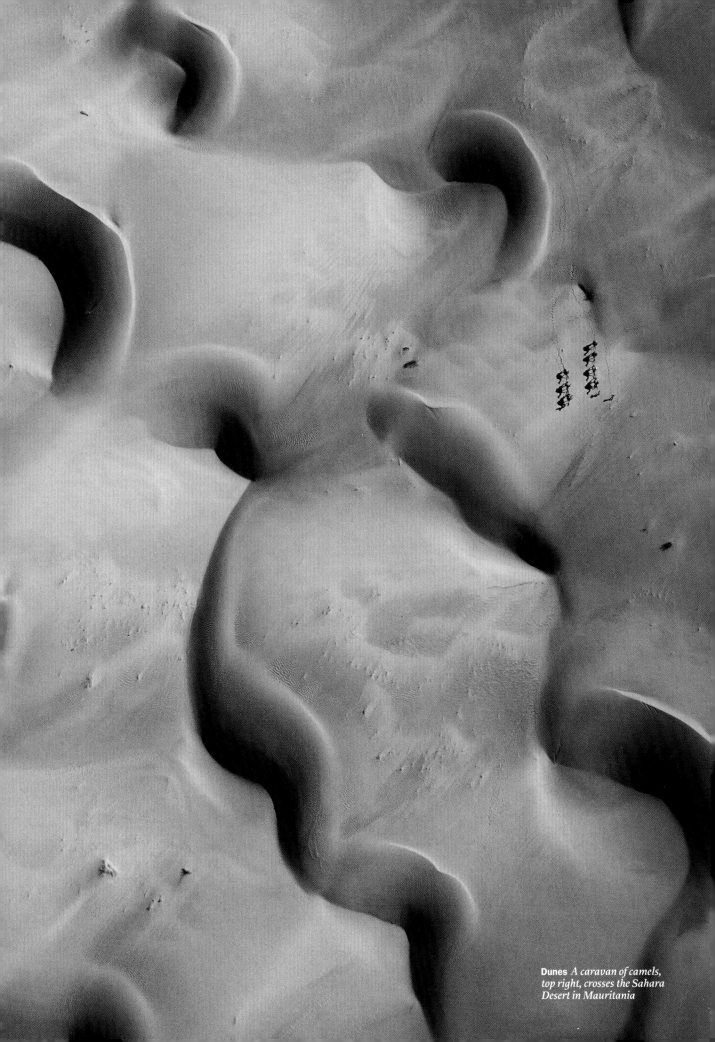

Dunes *A caravan of camels, top right, crosses the Sahara Desert in Mauritania*

It's a Mineral World

TO MANY OF US, MINERALS ARE ANYTHING THAT isn't animal or vegetable, and rock is what beats scissors but loses to paper. Scientists require a tad more precision, however, so here goes: minerals are nonliving substances, usually occurring in crystal form, that are manufactured naturally by the earth's geological processes, chiefly heat and pressure. They consist of either a single element in pure form, such as the carbon that makes up diamonds, or of multiple elements bonded together into a single, stable molecular compound, like quartz, which is composed of bonded silicon and oxygen. As for rocks, they are the mutts of the mineral world: less pure, they consist of pretty much a hodgepodge of various mineral compounds.

The essential truth about minerals is that we need them to survive. Our bodies would stop functioning in a matter of days if the foods we eat were suddenly depleted of the dozen-plus minerals, such as calcium, sodium and iron, that help us stay alive, from supplying the raw material that builds our bones to regulating fluid levels within each of our cells.

The minute doses of minerals our bodies require each day are measured in milligrams, but the quantities needed by modern societies every 24 hours are expressed in billions of tons. Even if humans can exist for several days without minerals, modern human society would likely grind to a halt within hours of being deprived of the 40-plus minerals that go into every telephone, the 35 needed to make a TV set and the 15 built into an average car. Without quartz, the most common mineral found in the planet's crust, computers, lasers, radios and most timepieces would cease to function immediately. And farmers worldwide would hang up their hoes if the vast quantities of phosphate used in fertilizer were unavailable.

Rock, if less elemental, is just as essential. Nature manufactures it in three ways: igneous rock forms when volcanic magma solidifies; sedimentary rock results when particles of minerals are deposited by the action of water or wind and are compressed over millions of years; and metamorphic rock, the fun stuff, is made by subjecting either of the first two types to additional heat and pressure over long periods of time.

Marble, that graceful metamorphic rock, forms when sedimentary deposits rich in calcium carbonate recrystallize under intense weight and heat. When polished, its surface is easily penetrated by light, giving it a luminous shimmer. Gemstones brighten our lives and are often the most precious gifts we bestow. And limestone, a sedimentary rock, is the very stuff history is made of: it is the backbone of buildings from the Pyramids to the Parthenon. Call it the rock of ages. ■

Limestone and Quartz

At left is a purple amethyst, a form of quartz, that was created within a geode, a roundish rock that occurs in sedimentary and some volcanic rock formations. A geode's exterior is usually limestone; its interior contains either quartz or chalcedony.

At right is an eroded limestone pinnacle at New Zealand's Cathedral Cove. A hard sedimentary rock, limestone is often the last type of stone to erode in landscapes primarily composed of sedimentary rock.

Giant Steps

OUR WORLD IS SHAPED BY CERTAIN INEXORABLE LAWS OF physics, mathematics and geometry. But nowhere is the work of nature as mathematician more apparent than in the marvelously geometric geology of the rock formations dubbed Giant's Causeway on the coast of County Antrim in Northern Ireland. Here, along a rugged coastline of the Irish Sea, some 40,000 basalt columns march into the waves, with each column composing a strongly geometric shape. The majority are hexagons, but there are also columns with four, five, seven and eight sides, clustering in a honeycomb pattern and thrusting as high as 36 ft. (11 m) into the sky.

The columns were formed following volcanic eruptions some 50-60 million years ago, when molten basaltic lava cooled, then fractured along strict mathematical lines as it hardened, forming straight edges as sharp as those seen in quartz formations. While Giant's Causeway may be the most singular example of volcanic geometry, it is by no means unique. Devil's Tower National Monument in Wyoming, familiar as a landing pad for the "mother ship" in the 1977 film *Close Encounters of the Third Kind,* is a butte composed of similarly hardened magma, in this case porphyry, that rises a staggering 1,267 ft. (386 m) above the harsh plains around it. Other columns crafted by volcanic activity can be found across the globe, from Russia to the Azores to New Zealand.

As for the causeway's titular giant, he is none other than Finn McCool, the legendary Irish Goliath who supposedly built the columns as a bridge to Scotland. Had he crossed the Irish Sea for a visit, he would have found a similar basaltic formation on the Isle of Staffa: Fingal's Cave, which scientists believe was formed in the same round of volcanic activity that shaped Giant's Causeway. ■

Volcanic Columns of the World

Cyclopean Isles These Mediterranean islands, formed by a volcano and said to be the stomping grounds of Homer's Cyclops, may once have been attached to Sicily. Like those of Giant's Causeway, the columns here are primarily composed of basalt.

Devils Postpile This formation, exposed on a cliff face near Mammoth Mountain in eastern California, is very recent; it has been dated to sometime between 100,000 to 700,000 years old. The basalt columns here are large, soaring 60 ft. (18 m) high and averaging 2 ft. (0.6 m) in diameter.

Flores Island This isle in the western Azores is home of the prominent Rocha dos Bordhões, whose soaring, exposed cliff face is composed of vertical basalt columns.

Mount Cargill This long-dormant volcano in New Zealand sports tall basalt columns known as the Organ Pipes.

Staffa The basalt columns on this picturesque island in the Inner Hebrides of Scotland are close kin to those at Giant's Causeway. The isle's famed Fingal's Cave inspired a work by Mendelssohn.

rock formations

Rock Stars

GEOLOGISTS DIVIDE ROCKS INTO THREE TYPES. Igneous rock is formed from magma ejected by volcanoes. Sedimentary rock, which makes up a good deal of the planet's land surface, is formed by the slow buildup of particles carried by air, ice or flowing water. Metamorphic rock is formed when pre-existing igneous or sedimentary rocks are subjected to high heat or pressure, changing their physical and chemical makeup. But those jaw-breaking terms don't begin to do justice to the poetry of rocks, seen here in some of their most remarkable incarnations.

At left is Sunset Point at Bryce Canyon National Park in Utah, where erosion by wind, water and ice has shaped sedimentary rock into the exotic pinnacle formations known as hoodoos. A chemical reaction, the conversion of carbon dioxide by rain into a weak form of carbonic acid, is one agent in dissolving the limestone into these picturesque forms over millions of years.

The White Cliffs of Dover on Britain's southeast coast, which soar in places to 350 ft. (107 m) over the English Channel, are among the planet's most celebrated rock formations; they've weathered some changes over the past 140 million years or so. Originally seabeds formed by the sedimentary chalk deposits of the skeletons of millions of tiny sea creatures, they were covered by glaciers during the Ice Age. When the glaciers retreated, the cliffs were shaped by hydraulic erosion as ocean levels rose. Similar cliffs can be seen on coastlines in Denmark and Germany. Erosion continues at a rate of some 1 cm a year, although a large shard of the cliff face tumbled into the Channel in 2001. ∎

Tsingy de Bemaraha Strict Nature Reserve

The "forest" of limestone needles above is part of the unusual karst topography of the Tsingy de Bemaraha Strict Nature Reserve in Madagascar, which was named a UNESCO World Heritage Site in 1990. The term karst is derived from Kras, the region of Slovenia in which scientists first explored this unusual type of landscape, which is characterized by the dissolution of the surface layers of bedrock and the presence of sinkholes and extensive caves and water channels beneath the ground. Subterranean karst regions are often described as resembling a cutaway section of Swiss cheese.

The resulting landscapes can be spectacular: running streams disappear from the surface, only to reappear above-ground far away; sinkholes can suddenly open in the ground, sometimes dragging trees and man-made structures down into their maw; soil erodes to reveal rock outcroppings which, as in Madagascar, can then be eroded by weather to form all sorts of unusual formations. The limestone needles above are kin to the rock pinnacles in Bryce Canyon National Park at left; both were formed over millions of years as wind, rain and chemical agents eroded softer layers of surface rock to expose the harder layers beneath.

Rising tide *The Karakoram range, as part of the Himalayas, is still getting taller; it forms an elevated barrier that helps shape the monsoon season in South Asia*

Uplifting

WHEN CONTINENTS COLLIDE, SOMETHING'S GOT to give. In the case of the Karakoram Mountains at left, the continents that collided are situated atop two gigantic tectonic plates, the Indian Plate and the Eurasian Plate. In many such smash-ups, one plate slides beneath the other in a process called subduction. But in this case, the energy from the collision was directed into vertical lift, thrusting the planet's crust high into the sky and creating the globe's highest mountain range, the Himalayas. The Karakoram range is a northern extension of the Himalayas; it lies along the border of China, India and Pakistan, which is home to its highest peaks, including K-2, the world's second-highest mountain.

These mountains are young in geological terms: the collision that created them took place 40 million to 50 million years ago. And because the process continues, the Himalayas rise about .04 in. (1 cm) a year. Scientists have retrieved fossils from ancient oceans high up in these ranges, proof that at one time these steep mountainsides were horizontal seabeds.

Many of the world's great mountain ranges, from the Andes in South America to the Rockies in North America, were shaped by the convergence of tectonic forces. Like the Himalayas, the Rockies are young mountains, formed when the Pacific Plate smacked into the North American Plate some 15 million years ago. Older ranges, like the ancient Great Smoky Mountains in Tennessee, below, show their age: they are often eroded, smoothed by weather and covered with trees and vegetation. But mountains hot off the tectonic griddle are still raw, steep and jagged—that's what makes the Rocky Mountains, well, rocky. ∎

Caledonian Mountains were part of a range with America's Appalachians until continental drift separated them

A River Runs Through It

THE MOST IMPORTANT FACTOR IN THE CREATION OF the planet's great canyons is invisible yet everywhere apparent: time. Canyons are the glorious residue of the operation of an irresistible force, flowing water, against an erodible object, stone, over vast eras of time. The forces that formed the scene above can be stated as a simple equation: *Colorado River + gravity + rock x 17 million years = Grand Canyon.*

The process by which rivers carve through rock, drawn by gravity to seek sea level, is called downcutting. Ironically, the Grand Canyon in Arizona was created by a process of uplifting as well as downcutting. Like the rest of the surrounding region, this area is rising, thanks to tectonics, as the North American Plate, pushed by the Pacific Plate, slowly elevates the level of the Colorado Plateau. (The Rocky Mountains are another spectacular result of this process.) This uplifting process raises the velocity of the river, increasing its downcutting power and carving the river-

bed ever deeper within the walls of the canyon. The astonishing result: in some places the river is more than 1 mile below the top of the surrounding cliffs.

If the Grand Canyon is a work in progress, so is our understanding of it. When this book was begun, geologists estimated the canyon to be about 6 million years old. But on March 7, 2008, *Science* magazine published a study by a team of scientists from the University of New Mexico that determined the age of the canyon to be closer to 17 million years. Team leader Victor Polyak said the findings, made possible by newly improved radioactive dating techniques, surprised the research team. The study also found that the Grand Canyon formed as two separate gorges, with erosion occurring more slowly in the western section than in the eastern section. The two gorges came together to form the single canyon familiar to us around 6 million years ago, the geologists said, near the feature known as the Kaibab Arch. ∎

Grand Canyons

Canyons are better suited for marveling than measuring. Any number of nations claim to be the home of the earth's deepest, longest or widest canyon; such claims are often advanced by tourist agencies rather than scientists. The list below skips the ranking game and names a few of the planet's most picturesque gorges.

Cotahuasi Canyon, Peru The deepest canyon in the Americas is 2.1 miles (3.3 km) below its surroundings at some points.

Fish River Canyon, Namibia The Fish River that carved out this mammoth canyon in Africa is only intermittently active today, flowing mainly during the late-summer flood season.

Kali Gandaki Gorge, Nepal/ Tibet The Gandaki River that created this deep gorge in the Himalayas is even older than the mountains that surround it.

Verdon Gorge, France Known as much for its beauty as for its 12-mile (20 km) length, this deep canyon was carved by the Verdon River, whose name reflects its bright green color.

Yarlung Tsangpo Canyon, Tibet Formed by the river of the same name that drains the northern Himalayas, it is one of the world's deepest gorges.

Great Plains

THE PLANET'S GRASSLANDS CIRCLE THE GLOBE ALONG ITS temperate and tropical zones on both sides of the equator; in these wide-open spaces, millions of large animals make their home on the range . This big-sky country is known by many names: Americans call their broad Western prairies the Great Plains; Russians know their vast short-grass domains as the steppes; in South America, Argentina's gauchos herd steers on the pampas, while Colombia's vaqueros savor life on the llanos; Africans refer to their vast tropical grasslands as savannas. Perennial grasses and nonwoody plants are the dominant vegetation here; trees and shrubs can be present but are often confined into individual groves near running water.

Grasslands provide grazing ranges for much of the world's livestock, and though they are a naturally occurring phenomenon, many of them have now been partially shaped by human hands in order to keep them free of trees and shrubs. Such areas are called anthropogenic grasslands; some have been cleared of trees and stumps by farmers seeking room to plant, while others are burned by herders every year, who emulate wildfires sparked by lightning to keep trees out and grass thriving. The constant growth and decay of the wild grasses here, further fertilized by wildlife, create a rich, deep layer of topsoil that in some cases extends 20 ft. (6 m) below the amber waves of grain. ∎

Data Stream: Earth's largest annual animal migration occurs in the Serengeti Plains in equatorial Africa

• **The steppes of southern Eurasia stretch from the Black Sea to north China, near the Pacific Ocean**

Archaic Arbors

Black Forest, Germany

It is perhaps best known for its kitsch factor—cuckoo clocks, rich cakes and tales of the Brothers Grimm—but the Black Forest deserves better. One of the great surviving primeval forests of Europe, it straddles the continental divide in south-western Germany; raindrops that fall here wind up traveling to the Atlantic via the Rhine or the Black Sea via the Danube. The forest's great stands of pine and fir were already heavily logged before Dec. 26, 1999, when 100-plus-m.p.h. winds from the huge cyclone Europeans dubbed "Lothar" devastated hundreds of acres of its green realm.

Dehesa Forest, Extremadura, Spain

This ancient oak forest covers much of western Spain and eastern Portugal, largely unchanged since the days when the Romans remarked upon its splendors after they first arrived in Iberia. Now, as then, the Dehesa is home to the famed Iberian pig, as well as the truffles it snuffles for and other mushrooms the size of wagon wheels. The Dehesa's prevalent tree is an evergreen, the holm oak, *encina* to Spaniards. In 63 B.C., a Greek geographer wrote that a squirrel could climb a tree beside a beach in southern Spain and, jumping from oak branch to oak branch, travel north to the Atlantic coast without touching the ground.

Beech Forests, Slovak Republic

The primeval beech forests of the Carpathians were named to the U.N.'s list of World Heritage sites in 2007. Scientists say the 10 distinct sectors that make up the site represent an invaluable genetic reservoir of European beeches (*Fagus sylvatica*). Aside from their genetic value, the forests are eerily beautiful, seemingly the work of an arborist wing of the Art Nouveau movement. The beechnuts that fall from the trees in autumn are highly nutritious, while the beechwood itself makes fine barrels for aging beer—if the folks at Budweiser are to be believed.

Data Stream: Giant sequoias grow in the Northeastern U.S. but more slowly than in the West • Holm oak foliage

Redwood Forest, Yosemite National Park, U.S.

Undisputed monarchs of the tree world, giant sequoias can grow as tall as 307 ft. (93 m) high—roughly the size of a 30-story skyscraper—and can be as large as 29 ft. (8.8 m) in diameter. Their great age is a match for their size: the most ancient known sequoia, measured by its rings, is 3,200 years old. *Sequoiadendron giganteum* is an evergreen that reproduces through seed cones. In the late 19th and 20th centuries, these giants were routinely felled, their timber used for such petty purposes as matchsticks. Thanks to public outrage, many of their habitats are now protected. Concerned botanists also took them to Europe and cultivated them with success.

resembles holly leaves • Spaniards call the dark pigs of the Dehesa Forest *pata negra:* "black hoof"

Realms of Rain

HOTHOUSES OF THE PLANET, RAIN FORESTS ARE A TESTAMENT TO NATURE'S sheer fecundity. Humid, viny, choked with vegetation, filled with the cries of exotic animals, these rich regions are laboratories of life, teeming with thousands of permutations of plants and animals: there are some 6,000 species of insects in the Central American rain forest, 6,500 species of orchids in the Indonesian rain forest. The operative word here is *rain:* a rain forest is a region that receives 68 to 78 in. (173 to 198 cm) of rainfall a year.

High humidity and abundant water supplies are the engines driving the phenomenal fertility of the rain forest—and all those green leaves, scientists have come to realize, make rain forests one of the foremost carbon reservoirs on the planet. Filtering carbon dioxide out of the air and replacing it with oxygen, rain forests are the thermostats of the globe, regulating temperatures and weather patterns. The Amazon rain forest, the world's largest, may produce as much as 20% of the planet's oxygen supply.

These hothouses are also reservoirs of invaluable genetic material. Many of our most powerful drugs—including those that fight diabetes, heart disease, malaria and arthritis—are derived from rain-forest plants. More than 2,000 tropical-forest plants have been identified by scientists as having anticancer properties, yet less than 1% of tropical rain-forest species have been analyzed for their medicinal value. Preserving rain forests from the widespread and accelerating rate of deforestation that currently threatens them will be an urgent environmental priority of the 21st century. ∎

Andean Aviary
Scarlet macaws gather in Peru's Manú National Park, the nation's largest nature reserve, which is inaccessible by automobile. Scientists have identified more than 800 species of birds in this UNESCO World Heritage Site, almost as many as the total number found in North America. Though they cover less than 2% of Earth's total surface area, the world's rain forests are home to 50% of the planet's plants and animals.

Great Rain Forests

Most of the world's rain forests are tropical, but ocean currents and regional weather patterns also create rain forests in temperate climes, most notably in the U.S. Pacific Northwest.

Amazon rain forest
Area: 2.3 million sq. mi. (6 million sq km)
The largest tropical rain forest in the world spreads across the Amazon River basin and is home to thousands of rare species of animals, trees and plants.

Central African rain forest
Area: 1.2 million sq. mi. (1.9 million sq km)
Centered on the Congo River, these are the richest tropical rain forests in Africa; rare animals include the bonobo and the African forest elephant.

Central American rain forests
Area: 200,000 sq. mi. (520,000 sq km)
The isthmus between North and South America is home to several rich tropical rain forests whose higher reaches include fog-shrouded cloud forests.

Indonesian rain forest
Area: 540,000 sq. mi. (1.45 million sq km)
One of the world's largest tropical rain forests spreads across the islands of the Indonesian archipelago; it is home to orangutans and a wide variety of palms and orchids.

Madagascan rain forest
Area: 14,670 sq. mi. (38,000 sq km)
Lemurs and chameleons abound in the low-canopied tropical rain forest on the Masoala Peninsula of the island of Madagascar in the Indian Ocean.

Pacific Northwest rain forest
Area: 480,000 sq. mi. (1.2 million sq km)
The world's largest temperate rain forest relies on the Japan Current to bring warm water and weather to its northern location.

Going down *The Coca River in the highlands of eastern Ecuador takes a plunge at San Rafael Falls. This region of Ecuador's rain forest is temperate, owing to the high altitudes and cooler weather*

The Northern Plains

BEHOLD THE ARCTIC TUNDRA IN FULL FLOWER IN Canada's Yukon Territory during the region's all-too-brief summer season. The growing window is open for only 50 to 60 days here, and the warmest days in July peak at 55°F. Winter brings some of the harshest weather on the planet, with the average temperature hovering at a chilling –20°F. Some compare conditions here to those in a desert, for annual rainfall is a skimpy 6 to 10 in.

Unseen but dictating the appearance of the stark, treeless landscape is a layer of permafrost, subsoil that remains frozen year-round. This barrier of cold material prevents trees and larger shrubs from extending their roots into the ground, resulting in a close-cropped landscape in which low shrubs and some flowering plants pop above the mosses, sedges and lichen that make up the majority of the vegetation. The permafrost layer also keeps the scant rainfall on the surface; it accumulates in smallish ponds, bogs and marshes, as in this picture. Wind is another invisible but essential element in this landscape, sweeping across the flat, glacier-scraped plains with no trees to hinder its progress.

Tundra makes up a large part of the earth's land surface, roughly 20%. The vast majority of tundra lies in a rough perimeter along the edges of the Arctic Circle, but the conditions that create this unique ecological system are also present in some high mountain regions. Alpine tundra shares the frosty snap and dwarfish vegetation of Arctic tundra but generally has soil that drains better.

Who lives here? The Yukon, one of three vast territories that make up Canada's northland, ranges over some 186,000 sq. mi., but it is inhabited by only some 31,000 people, two-thirds of whom live in the territory's only major city, Whitehorse. Animals far outnumber humans here, with species ranging from smaller mammals to wolves, caribou and polar bears; most carry an extra layer of fat to ward off the chill. The bestiary of the tundra is constantly shifting, for the harsh conditions here dictate survival via either hibernation or migration. ∎

Data Stream: The word tundra comes from a Lappish and Russian term meaning "hill" • Tundra is a young

Jewel of the Tundra

A tiny mushroom peeps up from the thin soil layer of the tundra. Trapped in the permafrost, vegetation in the tundra typically freezes rather than decomposes after it dies, and it does not release the carbon dioxide (CO_2) taken in during photosynthesis. Tundra has thus been one of the planet's major carbon dioxide sinks. But as warmer temperatures worldwide heat the permafrost layer, more CO_2 is now being released, exacerbating the problem in a dangerous feedback loop.

area of the planet, formed as glaciers retreated after the most recent Ice Age, 10,000 years ago

Windy city *A series of barchans, or arc-shaped dunes, in the Yemeni area of the Empty Quarter shows the direction of the wind that shaped them: it blew from left to right, leaving the hollow arc downwind*

Empty Empire of Sand

OR CENTURIES, THE SOUTHERN SECTION OF the Arabian Peninsula has been known as the Empty Quarter. Of course, this vast arena of sand, which forms a rough oval as much as 1,000 miles (1,609 km) wide in some directions—the distance from New York City to Memphis—isn't empty at all, as scientists see it, though the infrequent appearance of humans, water, plants and other scenic relief makes for challenging sightseeing for the rest of us. There are no roads here, making the Empty Quarter one of the largest expanses of little-explored land on the map. Then there's the heat, always the heat: the thermometer can soar past the 130°F (54°C) mark on summer days and "cool down" to 85°F (30°C) at night. Small wonder, even Bedouin acclimated to high temperatures keep to the fringes of this inhospitable domain.

Not all deserts share the severity of the Empty Quarter, or Ar-Rub' al-Khali, in Arabic. Some, like the semiarid deserts of the U.S. Southwest, are bursting with color and filled with fascinating life-forms adapted to a region where freshwater arrives intermittently and in small portions: cactuses and succulents, birds and animals. The Empty Quarter is far harsher, one of the globe's ur-deserts. Indeed, geographers view

it as essentially an eastern extension of North Africa's great Sahara Desert; the two were divided long ago by tectonic activity that created the Red Sea, the long channel that turned Arabia, once part of Africa, into a triangular peninsula.

It's the absence of water, of course, that both defines the desert climate and limits plant and animal life. The Empty Quarter receives an estimated 4 in. (10 cm) of rain a year, less than half of the 9.8-in. annual minimum that scientists use to define a desert environment. Even so, that's more than the planet's driest desert, the Atacama, high in the mountains of Chile, where there is sometimes no measurable precipitation in a year.

Desert environments, like polar environments, make excellent geological museums, since the weather is so stable. In 1998 a team of scientists from the U.S. Geological Survey ventured into the Wabar region of the desert to study a meteorite impact area where three crater rims are visible from the ground. They reported that the meteorite's three parts weighed some 3,500 tons and smacked into the planet with the force of the atom bomb exploded at Hiroshima. They dated the impact to only 135 to 450 years ago; it's no surprise that there are no firsthand accounts of this event. ∎

Huddled masses *These barchan dunes are less clearly defined than those at top left, lacking the hollowed-out downwind arc. On the right and in the background of the photo, rocky ridges rise above the desolate landscape*

Xeroxed landscape
Sculpted by the wind, identically shaped dunes stretch to the horizon

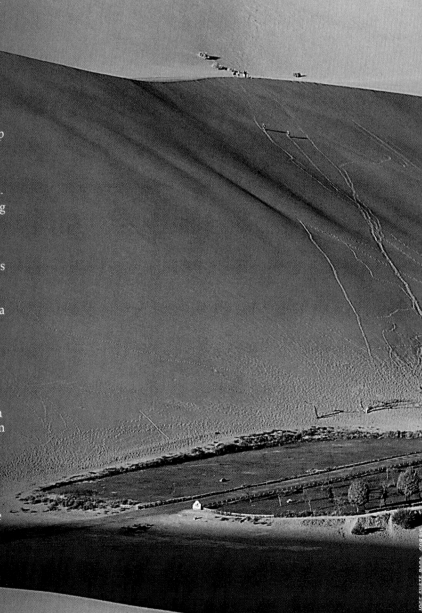

Mirage?

A SIGHT FOR WONDERING EYES, CRESCENT Lake, or Yueyaquan, nestles at the feet of the gigantic sand dunes of the Kumtag desert. This archetypal oasis, fed by an underground aquifer, is located about 3 miles (5 km) southwest of the city of Dunhuang (pop. 100,000) in the northwest province of Gansu in China. Centuries ago, Dunhuang was a major stop along the northern branch of the great Silk Road that linked China to the Middle East and Europe. But today both the city and the nearby oasis are threatened by desertification, the process by which formerly arable regions become more desert-like, unable to sustain human life.

The sands of the Kumtag are encroaching on Dunhuang at a rate of about 13 ft. (4 m) a year, and the city has seen its water table drop by 39 ft. (12 m) since 1975, while Crescent Lake's average depth has declined from 12 to 15 ft. (4 to 5 m) in 1960 to 3 ft. (0.9 m) today. Concerned Dunhuang officials are now limiting immigration to the city and are regulating farming and water-use practices.

Desertification is a growing threat all around the planet, driven by agricultural processes like overgrazing that strip nutrients from the land and deplete water resources, as well as by climate change that is increasing temperatures worldwide. The hardest-hit area is the Sahel region of Africa. This semiarid area along the southern fringe of the mighty Sahara desert has undergone severe drought and famine for decades, forcing millions from their homes as environmental refugees and creating severe social and political crises. A 2007 U.N. study found that some 50 million people will be threatened by desertification in the next 10 years, and an additional 2 billion may be uprooted by it in the future.

Meanwhile, in a local example of fiddling while Rome burns, newly affluent Chinese vacationers have made Dunhuang and Crescent Lake popular tourist attractions; the favored sport is sledding down the dunes. ■

Major Deserts of the World

Most scientists classify deserts as regions that receive less than 9.8 in. (250 mm) of rain a year. Hot deserts, like Africa's equatorial Sahara, have high temperatures year-round. Cold deserts, like the Gobi and the Kumtag desert, shown here, often lie at higher altitudes and undergo violent temperature fluctuations, with very cold weather prevailing during the wintertime. Both poles receive little rainfall, and technically the Antarctic and Arctic deserts are the world's two largest; below are the five next largest deserts, in order of size.

Sahara
Size: 3.3 million sq. mi.
(8.6 million sq km)
Location: North Africa

Arabian
Size: 900,000 sq. mi.
(2.3 million sq km)
Location: Arabian Peninsula

Gobi
Size: 500,000 sq. mi.
(1.3 million sq km)
Location: Mongolia, China

Patagonian
Size: 260,000 sq. mi.
(673,000 sq km)
Location: Argentina

Great Victoria
Size: 250,00 sq. mi.
(647,00 sq km)
Location: Australia

Source: TIME Almanac

cryosphere

cry·o·sphere (*n.*)
[Gk *kryo* cold, icy + Gk *sphaira* ball]
the portions of the earth's surface where water is found in
solid form, as in polar zones; the frozen world

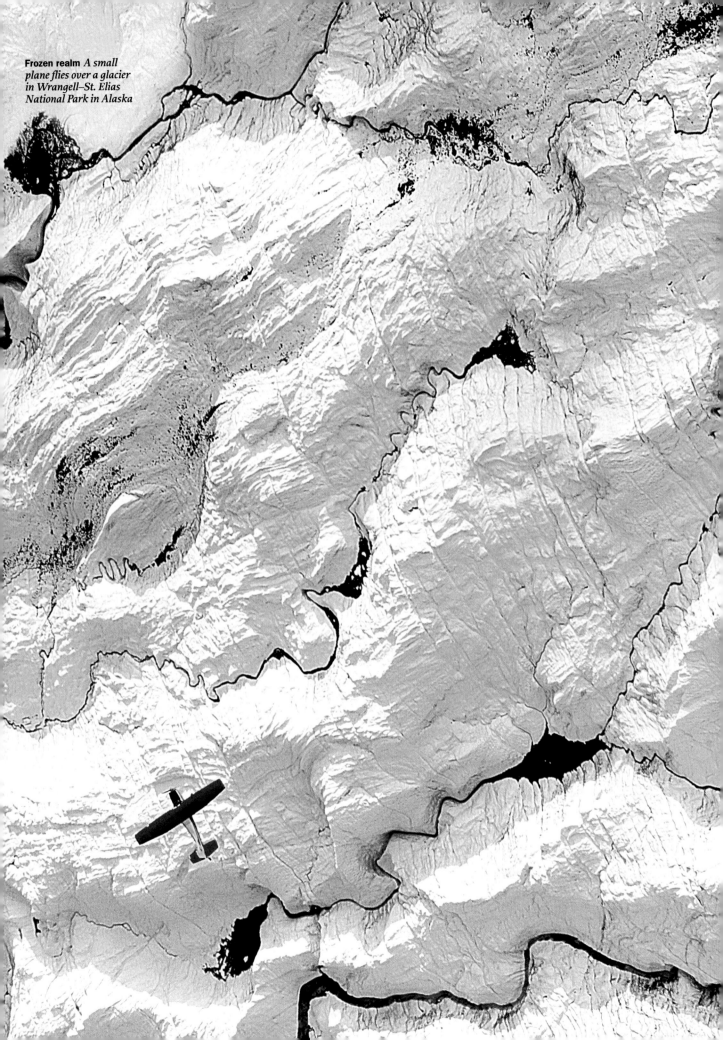

Frozen realm *A small plane flies over a glacier in Wrangell–St. Elias National Park in Alaska*

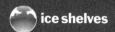

1/31/02   **2/23/02**   **3/7/02**

Breakup of the Larsen B Ice Shelf

Over a three-month period in 2002, the 600-ft. (183 m) -thick Larsen B Ice Shelf in Antarctica, which had been stable for more than 12,000 years, broke free of the glacier that formed it. Above at left, the shelf is dotted by dark-bluish melt ponds, indicating that collapse is imminent. In the middle photo, the shelf begins to crack free of land. In the third picture, it splin- *ters into thousands of iceberg slivers. The large area of light-blue ice in the 3/7 image may look solid, but it is composed of very closely packed icebergs and shards of ice that no longer are part of a coherent mass. The largest such collapse since the last Ice Age dumped 500 billion tons of ice into the ocean. The breakaway section was about the size of Luxembourg.*

Life on the Edge

PERCHED ATOP FRIGID POLAR SEAS, ICE SHELVES may look solid, but they are essentially objects in transition, part of the natural cycle of a polar glacier. These vast formations take shape when an expanding inland glacier drives its leading edge off of the land and out over the ocean, where it floats on the waters beneath it. This cantilevered platform of ice generally remains tethered to its parent glacier for years or decades (although some hang on for scores of centuries) before its length and weight cause it to break free, split into fragments and bob away on the waves. Denizens of the cryosphere, ice shelves exist in only three places: Greenland, Canada and Antarctica. The massive planes range in thickness from 150 to 1,200 ft. (46 to 366 m).

Ironically, the two facts many people think they know about ice shelves are wrong. First, the awe-inspiring 2002 breakup of the 1,200-sq.-mi. Larsen B Ice Shelf in Antarctica was not a direct result of global warming. Even some scientists initially got this wrong,

but an exhaustive 2008 study by Neil Glasser of Aberystwyth University in Scotland and Ted Scambos of the University of Colorado, published in the *Journal of Glaciology*, made a convincing case that climate change was only a contributing factor in the event. The fault lines that led to the collapse, they determined, were the result of decades-old crevasses created by long-term glaciological processes. Second, many people fear that the breakup and eventual melting of ice shelves will raise global ocean levels. They will not, for shelf ice is already floating in the water. Indeed, since frozen water takes up more space than the liquid kind, disintegrating ice shelves actually lower sea levels ever so slightly, when the calved icebergs travel to warmer waters and melt. But the disintegration of an ice shelf contributes indirectly to rising sea levels by removing the barrier to the glacier behind it. In such cases, the migration of ice from land to water—which does raise sea levels—can speed up by as much as eight times once the path has been cleared. ∎

Ice tray *The Ross Ice Shelf, above, is the largest such formation in Antarctica and is about the size of France. As with an iceberg, most of its mass lies below the water line*

Melting Away?

ARE WE LIVING THROUGH THE TWILIGHT era of the planet's great glaciers? The answer appears to be a resounding, alarming yes. A March 2008 study by the World Glacier Monitoring Service analyzed 100 inland glaciers across nine mountain ranges and found that the rate of global glacial shrinkage quintupled between 1980 and 2006. Why is this alarming? Because glaciers, despite their static appearance, are actually moving rivers of ice. They act as crucial reservoirs that store rain and snow, then steadily ration freshwater to rivers and streams, in small enough doses to prevent flooding but in large enough volume to quench the thirst of the surrounding landscape. Widespread glacial melting could reverse this balance, causing ruinous floods, followed by long droughts.

The problem is not limited to the comparatively small Alpine glaciers that roost atop mountains, far from the poles. A separate 2008 study (by the Institute of Arctic and Alpine Research) identified a second problem: faster melting also causes the large "continental" glaciers of Greenland and Antarctica, which store most of the world's freshwater, to slide more rapidly toward the ocean, where they calve into icebergs, float away and melt, further raising sea levels worldwide. The acceleration in the annual rate of ice loss in Antarctica alone may dump tens of billions of additional tons of frozen water into the oceans each year, a looming threat to millions of people living at sea level on the world's coastlines.

An ongoing long-term study by the National Snow and Ice Data Center, which compares the current size of the world's 3,000 major glaciers with that in historic photos, also indicates that the blanket of ice that covers 10% of the earth's surface is rapidly shrinking. Many scientists now believe that the Arctic Circle will be ice-free, at least during the polar summer, starting sometime around the year 2030. ■

MAIN IMAGE: URIEL SINAI—GETTY IMAGES; INSET LEFT: JAMES BALOG—AURORA PHOTOS; RIGHT: ANDREW C. REVKIN—THE NEW YORK TIMES—REDUX

From Ice to Water

Glaciers around the world are in headlong retreat, and the pace of this melt-off is no longer, well, "glacial."
The picture at left shows areas of light-blue meltwater where the surface of a glacier in Greenland is melting.
At right, a glacier in western Greenland is retreating up a valley, leaving a bare patch of ground in its wake.
In some cases, the meltwater can form into flowing streams, as shown in the main picture on these pages, also
taken in Greenland. Meltwater also penetrates cracks that run deep within the ice, eventually making its way
to the ground, where it acts as a lubricant, causing glaciers to slide more quickly toward the sea.

Data Stream: **Greenland icebergs survive for an average of three years** • **Icebergs can move as fast as 10 mile**

More than meets the eye *A newly-calved iceberg takes to the waters off Ilulissat, Greenland*

Things Unseen

WE'VE ALL HEARD THAT MUCH OF AN ICEBERG'S mass is concealed beneath the water. But seeing is believing, and this photo taken off the western coast of Greenland is a convincer. There are only two iceberg factories on Earth, Greenland and Antarctica, but they are prolific: more than 15,000 of the beautiful, dangerous objects calve from glaciers and cast off to sea each year. Icebergs float for the same reason that ice cubes do: frozen water weighs exactly as much as the same amount of the liquid kind, but takes up more space. This means that ice is necessarily lighter than the water it displaces, and the ratio of an iceberg's overall size to the portion that is visible above the surface (about 8 to 1) corresponds precisely to the difference between the volume of water in its liquid and solid phases.

Icebergs that calve from the Greenland glacier are believed to have been frozen about 15,000 years ago, but Antarctica's can be up to 10 times older. Greenland's icebergs are usually shaped like mountains, while Antarctica most often creates flat, "tabular" bergs. One recently discovered attribute of icebergs is that they "sing"—not in a manner that's audible to human ears but nonetheless real. In 2005, scientists monitoring earthquakes in Antarctica picked up low-frequency signals that seemed to move around with large icebergs. When the recording of these signals was sped up, they resembled everything from bees buzzing to the string section of an orchestra tuning up. The most widely accepted explanation for this effect is that icebergs develop a pervasive network of tiny cracks, through which water rushes at high speed, under intense pressure, causing the berg to vibrate and emit a sonic hum.

But the songs of icebergs may soon become golden oldies: the International Ice Patrol, which surveys the North Atlantic to prevent *Titanic*-style disasters, has often recorded as many as 2,000 bergs each year migrating south from the Arctic Circle. But in 2006, for the first time ever, they found not a single one. ■

a day • Ocean-floor gouges caused by ancient icebergs were found off North Carolina in 2007

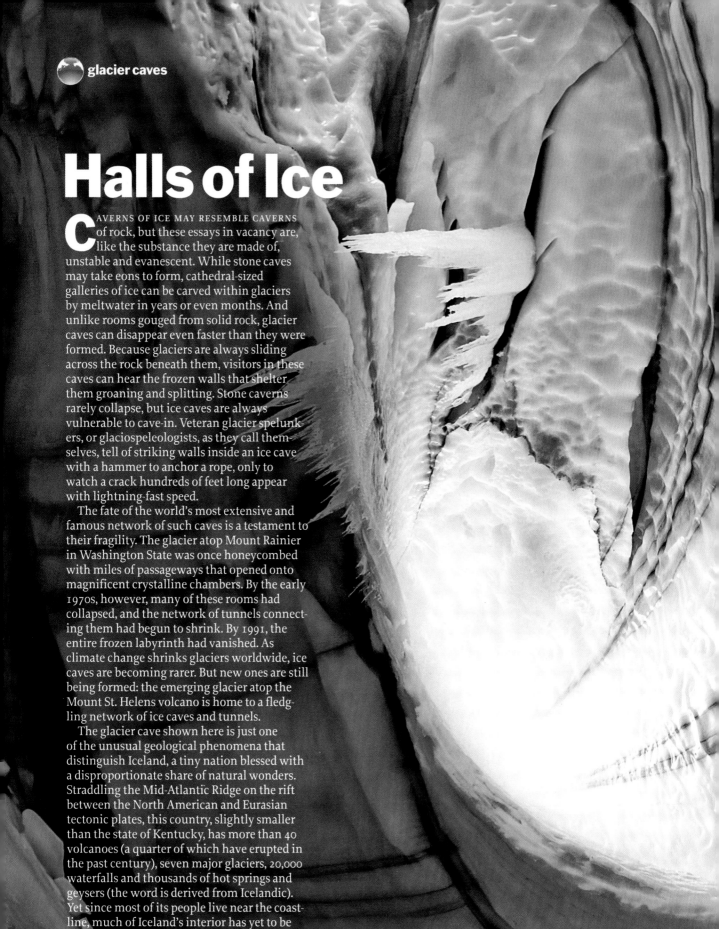

Halls of Ice

CAVERNS OF ICE MAY RESEMBLE CAVERNS of rock, but these essays in vacancy are, like the substance they are made of, unstable and evanescent. While stone caves may take eons to form, cathedral-sized galleries of ice can be carved within glaciers by meltwater in years or even months. And unlike rooms gouged from solid rock, glacier caves can disappear even faster than they were formed. Because glaciers are always sliding across the rock beneath them, visitors in these caves can hear the frozen walls that shelter them groaning and splitting. Stone caverns rarely collapse, but ice caves are always vulnerable to cave-in. Veteran glacier spelunkers, or glaciospeleologists, as they call themselves, tell of striking walls inside an ice cave with a hammer to anchor a rope, only to watch a crack hundreds of feet long appear with lightning-fast speed.

The fate of the world's most extensive and famous network of such caves is a testament to their fragility. The glacier atop Mount Rainier in Washington State was once honeycombed with miles of passageways that opened onto magnificent crystalline chambers. By the early 1970s, however, many of these rooms had collapsed, and the network of tunnels connecting them had begun to shrink. By 1991, the entire frozen labyrinth had vanished. As climate change shrinks glaciers worldwide, ice caves are becoming rarer. But new ones are still being formed: the emerging glacier atop the Mount St. Helens volcano is home to a fledgling network of ice caves and tunnels.

The glacier cave shown here is just one of the unusual geological phenomena that distinguish Iceland, a tiny nation blessed with a disproportionate share of natural wonders. Straddling the Mid-Atlantic Ridge on the rift between the North American and Eurasian tectonic plates, this country, slightly smaller than the state of Kentucky, has more than 40 volcanoes (a quarter of which have erupted in the past century), seven major glaciers, 20,000 waterfalls and thousands of hot springs and geysers (the word is derived from Icelandic). Yet since most of its people live near the coastline, much of Iceland's interior has yet to be fully explored, and many of its geological oddities are yet to be fully documented. ∎

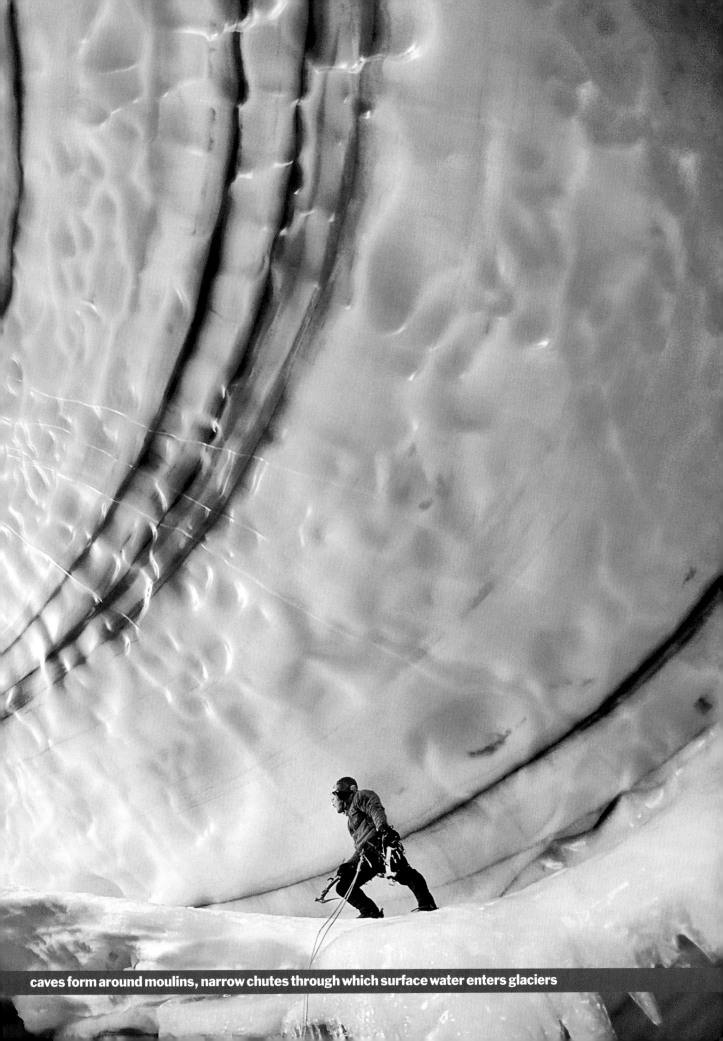

caves form around moulins, narrow chutes through which surface water enters glaciers

Bio-Snow?

WE'VE ALL HEARD THAT NO TWO SNOWFLAKES are identical. The notion may be more poetic than scientific, but it effectively makes its point: that nature is both staggering in its diversity and remarkable in its precision. Like the geometric basalt columns of Giant's Causeway in Northern Ireland or the regularity of the tides, the geometry of snowflakes reminds us that nature's actions, however unpredictable at times, are governed by basic laws of physics and mathematics. The crystalline symmetry of a snowflake reminds us that the white stuff is composed of ice crystals that combine to form different shapes of snowflakes, as influenced by local weather conditions, especially the temperature.

Snow, much like lightning, is such an everyday wonder that it's easy to forget that we still have much to learn about the mechanics that drive this basic form of precipitation. That was made abundantly clear by the publication in the Feb. 29, 2008, issue of the journal *Science* of new research on the origins of snow and rain. A team of researchers led by Brent Christner, professor of biological sciences at Louisiana State University, reported that bacteria swept off plants into the atmosphere may play a key role in the formation of rain and snowflakes, and thus in the entire cycle of precipitation that irrigates the planet.

Scientists have long known that water vapor in clouds needs something to cling to, a nucleus of sorts, in order to coalesce into raindrops or snowflakes. The new research shows that windborne bacteria may make up the largest percentage of these so-called nucleators. In snow samples taken from Antarctica, France, Montana, the Yukon and other locations, bacteria made up 85% of the nucleators in some cases. The new findings are further proof of the enormously complex mechanisms that keep our world turning. The team's findings supported an assertion first made years ago by a member of the group, David Sands of Montana State University, that the precipitation cycle should be renamed the bioprecipitation cycle. Said lead researcher Christner: "We are just beginning to understand the intricate interplay between the planet's climate and biosphere." ∎

TOP LEFT: VISUALS UNLIMITED—CORBIS; OTHER SNOWFLAKES: VISUALS UNLIMITED—GETTY IMAGES (8)

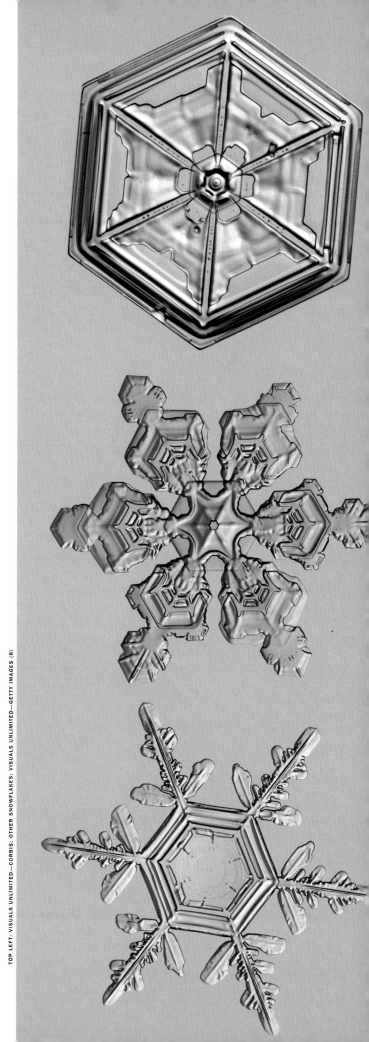

In Ice's Grip

BRINGING A TOUCH OF THE CRYOSPHERE TO YOUR BACKYARD, ice storms are the crystalline residue of a complex and relatively rare set of weather conditions. Ice storms begin to form when two layers of cold air (one near the earth's surface, another far above) corral between them a tier of warm air, which would normally hug the ground. When cloud-borne moisture is put through this three-part wringer, it gets a workout. Precipitation from the top layer starts out as snow, then falls into the middle, warmer belt, where it melts into rain. On its way through the lowest belt, the raindrops undergo a little-understood process known as "supercooling"—they are chilled well below the freezing point of water yet still remain liquid. When this unnaturally cold water hits the ground, which has also been cooled to the freezing point or lower, it instantaneously freezes into a translucent glaze that takes on, in intricate detail, the shape of whatever it surrounds.

If you've ever tried to chop this glazed ice off a sidewalk, you've probably noticed that it's much harder than the kind of ice that forms in a frozen puddle. This is not your imagination: the supercooling process expels impurities like dust from the droplets as they fall and also pushes almost all air bubbles out of the water. The result is the purest—and hardest—form of ice produced by nature.

It is also the most dangerous. As glaze ice accumulates on tree branches and power lines, it can cause both to collapse, blocking roads and depriving entire regions of electricity and heat. In short, not so supercool. Still, one of nature's most destructive disturbances is also among its most beautiful. Encased in a glistening crystal sheath, an iced-over world shimmers in sunlight and casts sparkling shadows in moonlight. In aesthetic terms, at least, an ice storm is nature's most perfect storm. ■

Data Stream: Ice-storm glaze is among the densest forms of ice on Earth • A 6-in. square of it a fraction of an

Nature the Glazier

Coating every surface in a heavy glaze, ice storms can send the limbs of trees like the beech at left crashing to the ground. A 1996 storm in Portland, Ore., shown on the left-hand page, caused massive damage and power outages. Above, an acacia leaf acquires a shell of glaze ice

geosphere

geo·sphere *(n.)*
[Gk *geo*-earth, land + Gk *sphaira* ball]
the solid earth, as distinguished from the hydrosphere
or atmosphere; one of the spheres or spherical layers within
the earth; the subterranean world

in transition *After an eruption at Volcanoes National Park in Hawaii, the surface of hot lava is cooling to form igneous rock while its interior is still glowing*

Inner Core The heart of the planet is thought be be a ball of iron or nickel kept in a solid state by the immense pressure around it. Some scientists think it is hotter than the surface of the sun

Upper Mantle Beneath the crust lies a layer of rock with the texture of pudding or clay

Lower Mantle This sphere of liquefied rock is the origin of the magma ejected from volcanoes that hardens to form new crust for the planet

Outer Core Deep inside the planet is this sphere of liquid metal, primarily nickel and iron. It spins as the planet rotates, providing its magnetic field

Crust The "skin" of the planet is about 50 miles (80 km) deep— and we have never seen or drilled below it

As the World Churns

ERMS LIKE *ROCK SOLID* AND *TERRA FIRMA* reflect the instinctive human belief that our planet is essentially both solid and static, but like many of the things that "everybody knows," this is very far from the truth. Starting as a mass of cosmic dust and debris that tried (and failed) to ignite into a star almost 5 billion years ago, our world has never quite lost touch with its turbulent roots.

With an inner core perhaps hotter than the surface of the sun, the planet continually recycles and reinvents itself. Humans, plants and animals are passengers aboard the giant tectonic plates that compose its crust. These huge structures carry the world's oceans and seas on their back, floating upon the mantle of molten rock and minerals that surrounds Earth's hard inner core. At one time a number of these plates were united, forming a single primordial supercontinent, Pangea. But around 180 million years ago, Pangea broke apart into more than a dozen pieces that drifted in every direction, ultimately to form the map we know today. As this process continues, some geologists believe that it will unite North America with Japan and China some 250 million years from now, while Australia may connect with Africa and Antarctica in about half that time.

In the scale of geologic time, Earth's contemporary surface is temporary indeed; the action of tectonic plates drags older land that has had its day in the sun down into the hot interior of the planet, where it is forged anew, destined one day to rise again. ■

GRAPHIC BY LON TWEETEN, TIME

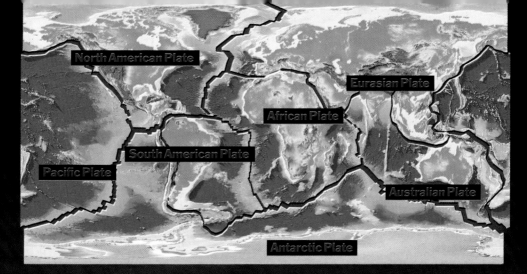

North American Plate

Eurasian Plate

African Plate

South American Plate

Pacific Plate

Australian Plate

Antarctic Plate

Tectonic Earth The planet's crust is made up of about 11 major tectonic plates and 20-odd smaller ones (scientists are still debating the numbers). We've shown only the seven largest plates in the graphic above. The plates float on the hot upper mantle of the planet's core, which has the viscosity of Silly Putty. Like lily pads covering the surface of a pond, these vast structures jostle against one another, creating enormous shocks that lead to earthquakes and tsunamis. When the plates collide, one sometimes wedges above the other, forcing it down into the mantle in a process called subduction. That lower plate is then melted and recycled through volcanic action. At other times, the collision of two tectonic plates thrusts one plate high into the sky, a process that has formed such mountain ranges as the Himalayas and the Rockies.

(ILLUSTRATION NOT TO SCALE)

1. Deep-ocean trenches These gashes in the crust lie at the bottom of the ocean, where one tectonic plate is subducted beneath another. Shown: Japan's deep-sea exploratory vessel *Shinkai 6500*

2. Volcanoes Hot liquid rock, magma, is ejected from the planet's upper mantle in an eruption

3. Earthquakes Most quakes occur where the edges of tectonic plates come together

4. Tectonic rifts The borderlines where plates meet are earthquake-prone. Shown here: the San Andreas Fault in California

5. Geysers Water heated by the planet's crust is ejected, often to cool, reheat and erupt again

The Great Divides

VISIONARY ARCHITECT BUCKMINSTER FULLER crafted an eye-opening metaphor when he urged us to regard our planet as Spaceship Earth. But when it comes to the geological forces that shape our world, it's helpful to think of the planet as Baseball Earth, with the zones where giant tectonic plates converge corresponding to the seams of the globe.

Alfred Wegener's theory of plate tectonics is the grand unifying theory of modern geology, explaining many of nature's most extreme processes, from earthquakes to volcanoes. Yet it's still mind-boggling to grasp the size of the forces involved, which operate over hundreds of millions of years of time and across the entire surface of the planet, land and sea alike.

Scientists now believe that the planet's "skin" is composed of 7-12 major tectonic plates (they're still arguing over definitions and numbers), as well as some 20 smaller plates, which float upon a layer of molten rock whose consistency resembles a stiff batch of tapioca pudding. The areas where these giant plates are moving away from one another are termed tectonic (or continental) rifts, and they make up the planet's most active geological zones.

The famed "ring of fire," the necklace of volcanoes that traces the perimeter of the Pacific Ocean, marks the areas where the Pacific Plate meets several other plates. The Pacific Plate bumps up against the North American Plate in mid-California, in the earthquake-prone zone called the San Andreas Fault. The other end of the North American plate rubs against the Eursian Plate in Iceland: the meeting of these seams of Baseball Earth creates the spectacular scene below. ■

Data Stream: The Red Sea lies where the Arabian and African plates are drifting apart • Tectonic plates are

Planet Seams *At left, the continental rift at Thingvellir was the site of the Icelandic Althing, or parliament, in the 10th century. Below, the San Andreas Fault cleaves the ground in San Luis Obispo County, Calif.*

Cracking Up, Bigtime

ARE YOU READY FOR THIS?" U.S. GEOLOGICAL SUR-vey seismologist Tom Brocher asked a meeting of California emergency-preparedness officials during a March 2008 conference. "I hope you are," he continued, "because this earthquake is ready for you." He was referring to a series of studies published in early 2008 that attempted to predict how bad the next major earthquake to occur in the San Francisco Bay Area will be, and when it will hit.

Here's how bad, according to Brocher: the temblor scientists believe is coming can be expected to disable (or knock over) the San Francisco–Oakland Bay Bridge, rupture the Hetch Hetchy Aqueduct that supplies most of the city's drinking water, wreck 90,000 homes, turn 220,000 people into refugees and cause an unknown number of deaths and injuries. Damages are projected to run to many tens of billions of dollars.

And here's when: recent excavations along the Hayward Fault Zone, where the North American Plate brushes against the Pacific Plate, just east of San Francisco Bay, show that quakes of the magnitude required to cause this kind of chaos have historically hit once every 160 years. Over the past five centuries, though, this pace has quickened to 140 years. The last major Hayward quake was recorded in 1868—yes, 140 years ago. (The catastrophic 1906 San Francisco quake was centered on a different fault line, the San Andreas.)

Most earthquakes occur along the boundary lines where one of the planet's tectonic plates meets another. But how often does Atlas shrug? More than 1,300 times each day, somewhere in the world, the ground trembles—but most of these events are so minor as to escape human notice. One in 5 is strong enough to detect without instruments, and once every three days or so, a location on the planet shakes violently enough to cause serious damage. In one three-week period in March 2008, for example, significant quakes struck New Zealand, Indonesia, the Philippines, Japan, China, Iran, Greece, Turkey, Britain, Chile and the U.S. There wasn't anything unusual about this rate of quake activity—except that fortune smiled in that all of them took place in sparsely populated areas.

On March 20, 2008, a quake measuring 7.2 on the moment-magnitude scale, the successor to the outdated Richter scale, rocked a sparsely populated area in western China. No deaths were reported. But when human luck runs out and a quake of this size hits a densely inhabited location, the result is catastrophe. The Oct. 8, 2005, 7.6-magnitude quake that struck in Kashmir along the India-Pakistan border killed more than 30,000 people in a matter of hours, and ensuing exposure, dehydration and lack of food killed some 45,000 more in the days and weeks that followed. ■

Catastrophe in Kashmir

At left, survivors of the massive 2005 earthquake huddle in the Pakistani city of Muzaffarabad, epicenter of the quake, where fully half of all buildings collapsed. Originating more than six miles (10 km) beneath the city, the quake was unleashed when the Indian and Eurasian plates of the earth's crust (whose upswelling created the Himalayan mountains) lurched past each other.

Fissures *The town of Meckering in Western Australia was almost entirely destroyed by an October 1968 quake that registered 6.9 on the Richter scale, then the standard for measurement. The event ruptured all major roads and railways nearby, including the Great Eastern Highway, shown here, leaving a crack 18 miles (29 km) long in the earth's surface. Some of the quake's effects are still visible 40 years later*

A Volcano on Venus

The same geological forces that drive the systems of Planet Earth are active throughout our solar system: scientists have now documented the presence of volcanoes on several nearby planets and moons. Jupiter's moon Io is home to a number of volcanoes that spout sulfur dioxide. The monster at left is Maat Mons on Venus, which towers 5 miles above the mean planetary radius of Venus, equivalent to sea level on Earth. NASA's Magellan probe, which orbited Venus from 1990 until 1994, found evidence of relatively recent volcanic activity on Maat Mons, tracing ash flows near its summit and northern flank. Maat Mons is one of the largest volcanoes now known in the solar system; Olympus Mons on Mars is five times larger.

Kilauea, Hawaii

Planet Ventilators

Fly Geyser, Black Rock Desert, Nevada

Like volcanoes and earthquakes, geysers and hot springs open windows upon the potent forces hidden beneath the skin of the planet; it's a happy by-product that the vistas that result are so colorful and fascinating. The American West offers one of the most picturesque displays of the heat beneath our feet, abounding in unusual formations created by hydrothermal activity, the heating of water by subterranean hot rocks. Fly Geyser, above, lies in the geyser-rich region around Black Rock Desert, the dry bed of an ancient lake. This formation is in part man-made: farmers drilling for water in 1916 tapped into a hydrothermal aquifer that flooded the area. In the 1960s the geyser itself began spouting; it does so in a constant stream, unlike geysers such as Old Faithful in Yellowstone National Park, whose vented water flows back underground, only to be reheated and released on a steady timetable. The three cone-shaped spouts above have formed over the years as emitted minerals solidify, and they are still growing. ■

Data Stream: Yellowstone National Park is home to some 300 geysers • The Grand Prismatic Spring

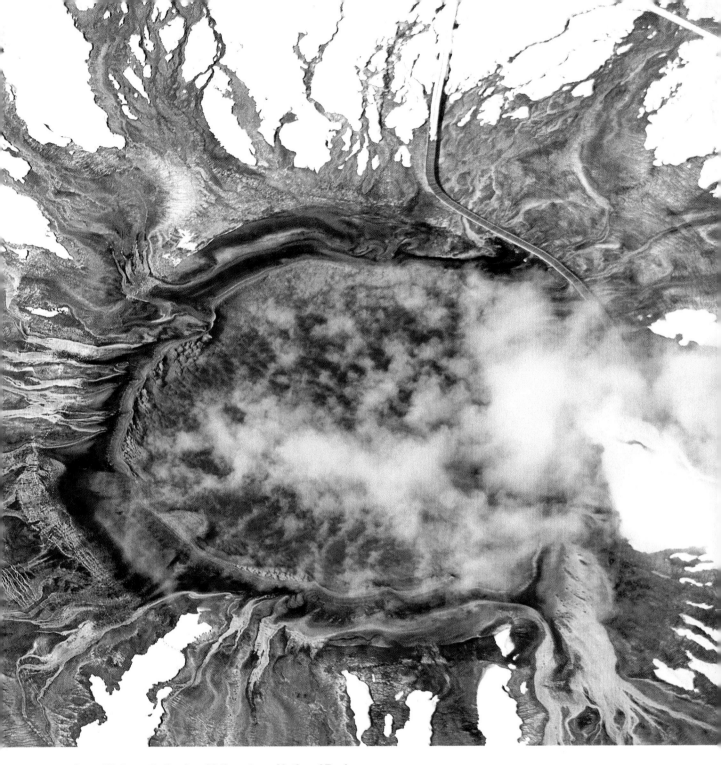

Grand Prismatic Spring, Yellowstone National Park

Hot springs are the products of the same hydrothermal power that creates geysers. The Grand Prismatic Spring at Yellowstone is one of the most striking of such formations, stretching from 250 to 380 ft. across. The third largest hot spring in the world, topped only by a pair of behemoths in New Zealand, it discharges 560 gal. of water a minute. The brilliant colors within the pool are not mineral deposits, though the spring is heavily laden with minerals churned up from under the ground; they are algae attracted to the extreme heat of the water, which ranges between 147°F and 188°F. Such heat-seeking life-forms are called thermophiles. Yellowstone National Park lies within the caldera of the relatively recent eruption of a volcano so large scientists call it a super-volcano; its eruption some 600,000 years ago may have been 2,500 times more powerful than the eruption of Mount St. Helens in 1980. The caldera is some 35 miles wide, so big as to escape detection until seen in satellite photographs in the 1960s. ■

changes hues with the seasons as different-colored algae bloom • The spring is 160 ft. deep in its center

Wonder Down Under

PORTALS TO THE UNDERWORLD, CAVES ARE READY-made geology labs, where processes generally unseen are exposed, vast eons of history are recorded, and nature, for a change, adorns a vacuum. Most caves are created by the undergound erosion of limestone due to the effects of a slightly acidic solution of water over vast stretches of time; they are called solutional caves. In their early stages of development, such caves are created by trickling groundwater, which gradually forces cracks and fissures in the limestone. The process is often accelerated as the new voids beneath the ground connect with rivers and springs, in some cases forming long tubes and vast subterranean chambers. In some older solutional caves, the water table that shaped the void has fallen, leaving the space dry. A different type of cave is formed through volcanic activity, when "bubbles" of space are preserved intact as molten lava hardens; they are called primary caves.

The glories of this netherworld are stalactites and stalagmites, formed by the slow trickling of ground-water saturated with calcium carbonate. Stalactites are the needles that hang from the ceiling; stalagmites "grow" from the floor as drops of calcium carbonate accumulate. Amid these eerie, beautiful formations, early men gathered in the firelight, for these quiet chambers are also the wombs of human society. ∎

Great Caves of the World

Carlsbad Cavern Famed for its abundance of ornate and spectacular formations, this cavern in the mountains of New Mexico is 31 miles (50 km) long.

Gunung Mulu Some of the earth's largest subterranean passages can be found in this important system in Sarawak on the island of Borneo in Malaysia, first entered in 1978 by British cavers. Its centerpiece, Sarawak Chamber, is the world's largest underground space: ½ mile (0.6 km) long, 1,300 ft. (415 m) wide and 330 ft. (100 m) high. The cave system itself is more than 200 miles (320 km) long.

Mammoth Cave The name isn't hype: this immense system in karst-rich Kentucky is easily the longest cave system in the world, at some 352 miles (566 km).

Optimisticeskaya This 132-mile (212 km) -long cave system in western Ukraine is distinctive for having been formed not out of limestone but out of gypsum.

Sistema Huautla The running streams that helped shape this cave system high in the Sierra Mazateca range in Oaxaca, Mexico, are still very active, and some of its flooded zones remain unexplored. The system is 39 miles (63 km) long.

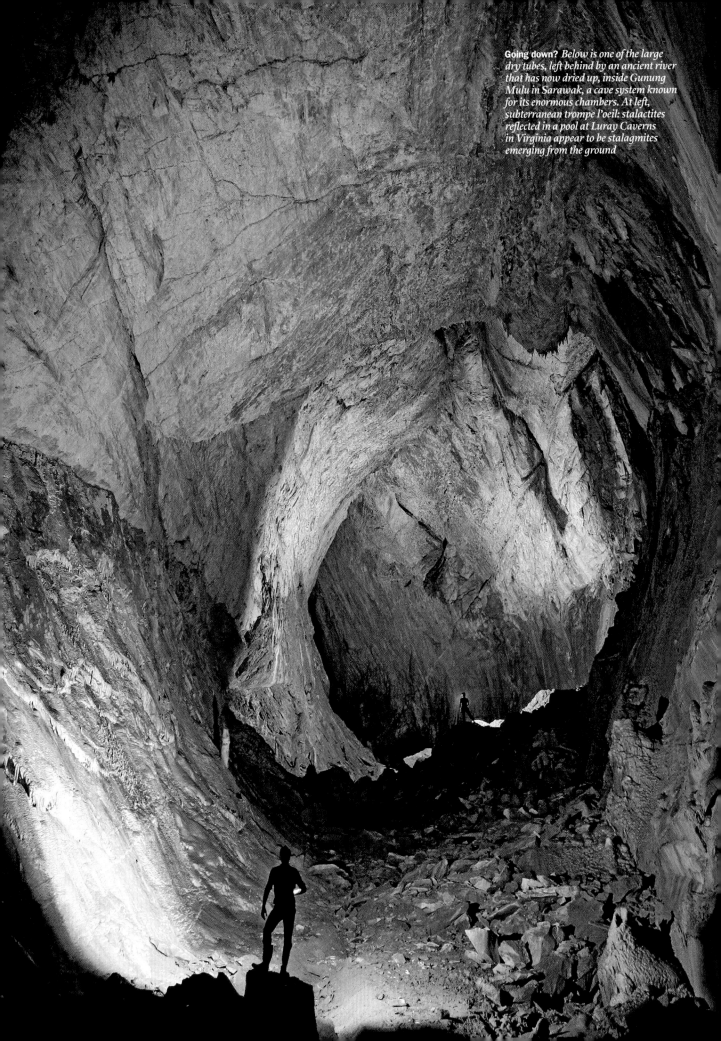

Going down? *Below is one of the large dry tubes, left behind by an ancient river that has now dried up, inside Gunung Mulu in Sarawak, a cave system known for its enormous chambers. At left, subterranean trompe l'oeil: stalactites reflected in a pool at Luray Caverns in Virginia appear to be stalagmites emerging from the ground*

A Room with a View

CENOTES ARE AMONG NATURE'S MORE WHIMSICAL creations. These underground hideaways are part cave, part lake, part swimming hole—and entirely beguiling. In truth, however, a cenote is essentially a glorified sinkhole, one that resembles a cave, contains a pond or lake of groundwater and often opens to the surface above. The planet's greatest trove of them lies in Mexico, particularly on the Yucatán Peninsula, but cenotes are also found on some Caribbean islands and in Australia. The term *cenote* is derived from the Maya and refers to a site where

groundwater can be found. Indeed, since the Yucatán has relatively few lakes and rivers, Maya settlements were often built near cenotes, which offered supplies of freshwater. The Maya capital of Chichén Itzá was built around an extensive network of them.

Cenotes form in areas of karst topography, when rock below the surface dissolves, creating a void covered by a thin layer of rock, soil and vegetation and filled with rainwater infiltrating through the ground. (Many cenotes are closed systems that are not fed by underground rivers or springs.) When the thin roof

Looking up *A visitor contemplates the view from the bottom of a cenote near Valladolid, Mexico*

The Stages of a Cenote

There are several distinct stages in the life of a cenote. The aerial photograph below, taken outside Tamulipas, Mexico, shows three sinkholes that may someday become cenotes. The two lower sinkholes have collapsed below the surrounding landscape; it is possible that only a thin layer of surface soil is acting as the ceiling of a more extensive vertical void directly beneath them, but it's also possible that the sinkholes have reached their maximum depth and will never become true underground cenotes. The shallow sinkhole at the top has already filled with water.

The extensive system of cenotes at Chichén Itzá was first explored by American Edward Herbert Thompson. In 1904 he began excavating the Sacred Cenote, a primary site of Maya religious worship, and found a number of ritual objects as well as human skeletons, suggesting that the cenote was used for human sacrifice. Today cave divers continue to explore the underground passages and byways of a large system of interconnected cenotes along the east coast of the Yucatán Peninsula in the state of Quintana Roo.

covering the underground void collapses, it becomes open to the surface, allowing rainwater to fall directly into the cavern. In later stages, cenotes can become filled with sediment and eroded soil and rock, until the waterline is covered and the cavern becomes a ravine. But geology lessons can't convey the sheer beauty of these entrancing, hushed spaces, alive with the trickle of water, shot through with shafts of sunlight dappling the long vines that dangle from the surface above and sometimes echoing with the oohs and ahhs of delighted human intruders. ■